T0268493

www.ingramcontent.com/pod-product-compliance
Lightning Source LLC
Jackson TN
JSHW061934140125
77097JS00004B/9

9780874417449

Season of Renewal

A FAMILY HAGGADAH

הגדה של פסח

By Rabbi Dr. John Levi and Naomi Tippett

Behrman House, Inc.
www.behrmanhouse.com
www.behrmanhouse.com/seasonofrenewal

For Noa and Zak, Savannah and Jarrah, Jordan and Elli,
Joshua, Amy, Lili, and grandchildren everywhere

— Naomi Tippett

Edited and interpreted by: Rabbi Dr. John Levi
Creative director: Naomi Tippett
Designer: Stacey May
Project manager: Dena Neusner
Editorial intern: Wilhelmina Roepke
Illustrators: Children from the King David School, Melbourne, Australia

Editorial committee:
Rabbi Martin S. Cohen
Rabbi William Cutter
Rabbi Daniel G. Zemel
Rabbi Fred Morgan
Rabbi Mottel Gutnick
Shayndel Samuel
Rabbi Aviva Kipen

Adapted from *A Family Haggadah,* previously published by Melbourne Books, Australia.

Published by Behrman House, Inc.
Millburn, NJ 07041
www.behrmanhouse.com
ISBN 978-0-87441-744-9

Library of Congress Cataloging-in-Publication Data

Haggadah. English & Hebrew.
Season of renewal : a family Haggadah / by John Levi and Naomi Tippett.
p. cm.
"Adapted from A Family Haggadah, previously published by Melbourne Books, Australia."
ISBN 978-0-87441-744-9
1. Haggadot--Texts. 2. Seder--Liturgy--Texts. 3. Judaism--Liturgy--Texts. 4. Haggadah. I. Levi, John. II. Tippett, Naomi. III. Title.
BM674.643.L48 2010
296.4'5371--dc22

2009039868

Manufactured in the United States of America

Acknowledgments:

Dedication and talent have been invested in this haggadah. There are so many who can be proud of their contribution.

First, Rabbi Dr. John Levi for his tireless work and inspiring interpretation of the text; the King David School, Melbourne, for their cooperation in the realization of this haggadah; the children of the King David School for their imaginative illustrations; Savannah Kron Jurvis for her additional artwork; David Tenenbaum of Melbourne Books, who has shown such faith in this haggadah; and my husband, George, for his thoughtful support.

I thank them all. This haggadah is testimony to their talent and enthusiastic participation.

— Naomi Tippett

Why This Haggadah?

Passover is a season of renewal—a return to spring, a chance to clean the leavening and dust from our lives and give ourselves a fresh, new start. It is also a time for us to affirm our commitment to our faith by following ancient traditions, sometimes with modern adaptations, as we share a joyful holiday meal with family and friends.

This haggadah is designed for families with children of all ages. Clear headings and straightforward directions make it easy to follow along. Intriguing facts and questions encourage participation and enhance understanding.

Passover is a multisensory experience. We see the flickering light of the advancing holiday, we taste bitterness, and we hold redemption and deliverance (through symbolic cups of wine) in our hands. We remember the past and look to the future; we tell stories and sing songs. A musical note ♫ appears next to songs that are available for free download at **www.behrmanhouse.com/seasonofrenewal**.

Enjoy the cheerful, blossoming artwork. Sing along to the lively songs. Learn something new. And may you have a joyful and meaningful Passover.

♫ Passover songs, performed by children from the King David School in Melbourne, Australia, are available for free on www.behrmanhouse.com/seasonofrenewal.

Rise up my love,
My fair one, come away!
For lo! the winter is past,
The rain is over and gone,
The flowers appear on the earth,
The time of singing has come,
And the song of the dove
Is heard in our land.

(Song of Songs 2:10-12)

Before the Seder

There are many ways participants can prepare for the seder in advance, to make the experience more meaningful. Children can practice the Four Questions, learn the Passover story, or create holiday artwork such as a matzah cover or seder plate. Adults can share *ḥaroset* recipes, gather photos of family members who will not be present at the seder, or prepare a skit or personal story about Passover. You might want to distribute the activities and discussion topics at the end of this haggadah a week or two before the seder, and invite participants to listen to Passover songs at **www.behrmanhouse.com/season of renewal** to encourage lively participation during the seder. You could also look through the rituals and readings in this haggadah in advance, and think about which parts the leader will read and which parts participants might take turns reading aloud.

By planning ahead, you can ensure that your seder will be a night unlike all others.

Seder Checklist

- The seder plate
- At least two candles, and matches
- A haggadah for each participant
- Wine glasses
- Wine and/or grape juice
- Three *matzot* (plural of matzah), and matzah cover
- Small bowl of salt water
- Cup, basin, and towel for handwashing
- Pillows for reclining
- Elijah's Cup, to be filled with wine
- Miriam's Cup, to be filled with water *(optional)*
- Flowers, centerpieces, handmade art *(optional)*

The Seder Plate

The symbols of the seder are arranged on a plate in the center of the table.

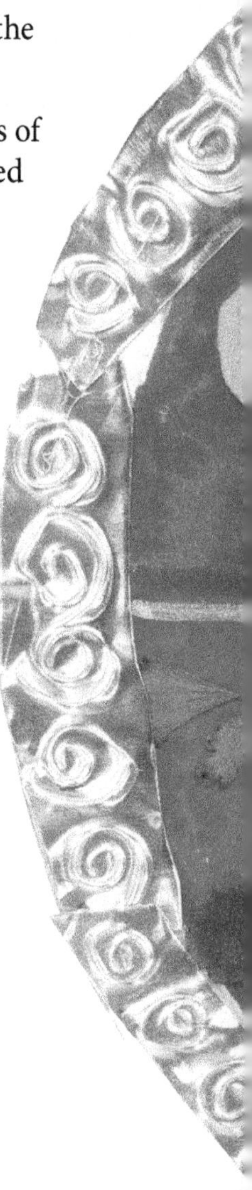

זְרוֹעַ *Zeroa* — A roasted bone (usually a roasted shank bone) to remind us of the Pesaḥ offering. Vegetarians sometimes use a beet.

כַּרְפַּס *Karpas* — Usually a green vegetable, like parsley or celery, that reminds us of spring. Those of Eastern European descent sometimes use boiled potatoes.

חֲרוֹסֶת *Ḥaroset* — A mixture of ingredients meant to symbolize mortar, a reminder of the bricks the Israelite slaves were forced to make. It is typically made from apples, chopped nuts, spices, and wine. Other ingredients such as dates, figs, apricots, oranges, and even bananas can also be used.

מָרוֹר *Maror* — A bitter herb, usually horseradish, to remind us of the bitterness of slavery.

בֵּיצָה *Beitzah* — A roasted egg, a symbol of new beginnings and of the sacrifices that were offered at the Temple in Jerusalem.

חֲזֶרֶת *Ḥazeret* — Some people put a second bitter herb on the seder plate, such as romaine lettuce, whose root is bitter.

מֵי מֶלַח Salt water — Some people put a bowl of salt water on the seder plate. We dip the karpas in salt water to remind us of the tears our ancestors shed in Egypt.

Some families place an orange on the seder plate as a symbol of the fruitfulness for all Jews when we accept and include *all* members of the Jewish community. If you could add a symbolic object to the seder plate, what would it be?

The Search for Leaven

The night before the seder we clean out the *ḥameitz* from our home. Invite children to help, and explain that ḥameitz is food that is made with an ingredient such as yeast that causes the food to rise. Ḥameitz includes bread, pasta, and many cakes and cookies.

We say a blessing as we begin the search for ḥameitz:

בָּרוּךְ אַתָּה, יְיָ אֱלֹהֵינוּ, מֶלֶךְ הָעוֹלָם,
אֲשֶׁר קִדְּשָׁנוּ בְּמִצְוֹתָיו, וְצִוָּנוּ עַל
בִּעוּר חָמֵץ.

Baruch Atah, Adonai Eloheinu, Melech ha'olam, asher kid'shanu b'mitzvotav v'tzivanu al bi'ur ḥameitz.

Praised are You, Adonai our God, Ruler of the universe, who has made us holy by commanding us to remove all the ḥameitz.

Candle Lighting

We read together:

May light shine on us, on all Israel, and on all the world.

We light the candles, then cover our eyes and say or sing the blessing. If our seder is on Friday evening, we include the words in parentheses.

בָּרוּךְ אַתָּה, יְיָ אֱלֹהֵינוּ, מֶלֶךְ הָעוֹלָם,
אֲשֶׁר קִדְּשָׁנוּ בְּמִצְוֹתָיו וְצִוָּנוּ לְהַדְלִיק
נֵר שֶׁל (שַׁבָּת וְשֶׁל) יוֹם טוֹב.

Baruch Atah, Adonai Eloheinu, Melech ha'olam, asher kid'shanu b'mitzvotav v'tzivanu l'hadlik ner shel (Shabbat v'shel) Yom Tov.

Praised are You, Adonai our God, Ruler of the universe, who makes us holy with commandments and commands us to light the (Shabbat and) Festival candles.

The Seder Begins!

Seder means "order." These are the steps in the order of our seder. We sing the names of the steps in Hebrew or read together in English:

Kadeish: The Kiddush	קַדֵּשׁ
Ur'ḥatz: Washing Our Hands	וּרְחַץ
Karpas: Dipping the Greens	כַּרְפַּס
Yaḥatz: Breaking the Middle Matzah	יַחַץ
Magid: Telling the Story	מַגִּיד
Roḥtzah: Washing Our Hands	רָחְצָה
Motzi Matzah: Blessings for the Matzah	מוֹצִיא מַצָּה
Maror: The Bitter Herbs	מָרוֹר
Koreich: The Hillel Sandwich	כּוֹרֵךְ
Shulḥan Oreich: The Meal	שֻׁלְחָן עוֹרֵךְ
Tzafun: The Afikoman	צָפוּן
Bareich: Blessing after the Meal	בָּרֵךְ
Hallel: Psalms of Praise	הַלֵּל
Nirtzah: Concluding Our Seder	נִרְצָה

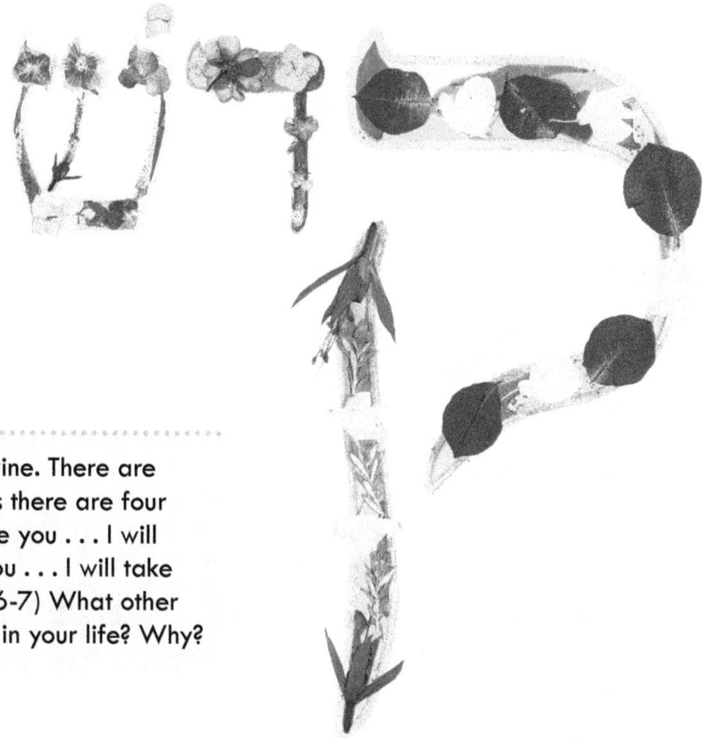

Kadeish: The Kiddush

Tonight we drink four cups of wine. There are four seasons of the year, just as there are four promises in the Bible: "I will free you . . . I will deliver you . . . I will redeem you . . . I will take you as My people." (Exodus 6:6-7) What other numbers have special meaning in your life? Why?

The First Cup of Wine

We fill the first cup of wine, and we each hold up our cup as we read together God's promise to our ancestors and to us:

אֲנִי יְיָ וְהוֹצֵאתִי אֶתְכֶם מִתַּחַת
סִבְלֹת מִצְרָיִם.

"I am Adonai, and I will free you from the burdens of the land of Egypt." (Exodus 6:6)

If Pesaḥ begins on Friday night, we start Kiddush with these words that come from the beginning of the Torah:

וַיְהִי עֶרֶב וַיְהִי בֹקֶר יוֹם הַשִּׁשִּׁי.
וַיְכֻלּוּ הַשָּׁמַיִם וְהָאָרֶץ וְכָל צְבָאָם.
וַיְכַל אֱלֹהִים בַּיּוֹם הַשְּׁבִיעִי, מְלַאכְתּוֹ
אֲשֶׁר עָשָׂה, וַיִּשְׁבֹּת בַּיּוֹם הַשְּׁבִיעִי,
מִכָּל מְלַאכְתּוֹ אֲשֶׁר עָשָׂה. וַיְבָרֶךְ
אֱלֹהִים אֶת יוֹם הַשְּׁבִיעִי, וַיְקַדֵּשׁ
אֹתוֹ, כִּי בוֹ שָׁבַת מִכָּל מְלַאכְתּוֹ, אֲשֶׁר
בָּרָא אֱלֹהִים לַעֲשׂוֹת.

There was evening and there was morning, a sixth day. When the heavens and the earth and all that they contain were completed on the seventh day, God finished the work that had been made, and God rested on the seventh day. And God blessed the seventh day and made it holy, because God rested from the work of creation. (Genesis 1:31-2:3)

On Shabbat and weekdays we sing together:

בָּרוּךְ אַתָּה, יְיָ אֱלֹהֵינוּ, מֶלֶךְ הָעוֹלָם,
בּוֹרֵא פְּרִי הַגָּפֶן.

Baruch Atah, Adonai Eloheinu, Melech ha'olam, borei p'ri hagafen.

Praised are You, Adonai our God, Ruler of the universe, who creates the fruit of the vine.

(On Shabbat, we add the words in parentheses.)

בָּרוּךְ אַתָּה, יְיָ אֱלֹהֵינוּ, מֶלֶךְ הָעוֹלָם,
אֲשֶׁר בָּחַר בָּנוּ מִכָּל עָם, וְרוֹמְמָנוּ
מִכָּל לָשׁוֹן, וְקִדְּשָׁנוּ בְּמִצְוֹתָיו, וַתִּתֶּן
לָנוּ יְיָ אֱלֹהֵינוּ בְּאַהֲבָה (שַׁבָּתוֹת
לִמְנוּחָה וּ) מוֹעֲדִים לְשִׂמְחָה, חַגִּים
וּזְמַנִּים לְשָׂשׂוֹן אֶת יוֹם (הַשַּׁבָּת
הַזֶּה וְאֶת יוֹם) חַג הַמַּצּוֹת הַזֶּה.
זְמַן חֵרוּתֵנוּ, (בְּאַהֲבָה) מִקְרָא קֹדֶשׁ,
זֵכֶר לִיצִיאַת מִצְרָיִם. כִּי בָנוּ בָחַרְתָּ
וְאוֹתָנוּ קִדַּשְׁתָּ מִכָּל הָעַמִּים. (וְשַׁבָּת)
וּמוֹעֲדֵי קָדְשְׁךָ (בְּאַהֲבָה וּבְרָצוֹן)
בְּשִׂמְחָה וּבְשָׂשׂוֹן הִנְחַלְתָּנוּ. בָּרוּךְ
אַתָּה, יְיָ, מְקַדֵּשׁ (הַשַּׁבָּת וְ) יִשְׂרָאֵל
וְהַזְּמַנִּים.

Praised are You, Adonai our God, Ruler of the universe, who has chosen us from among peoples and languages by giving us *mitzvot*. In love You have given us (Shabbat for rest and made) special times for happiness, holy days, and seasons for joy. (This Shabbat day and) this Festival of *Matzot* is our own season of freedom and the time for holy acts, reminding us about the Exodus from *Mitzrayim*, the land of Egypt. For you have chosen us and made for us times of happiness and joy. We praise You, O God, who gave us (Shabbat,) Israel, and the festival seasons.

Havdalah

On Saturday night we add the Havdalah prayers that set Shabbat apart from the other days:

בָּרוּךְ אַתָּה, יְיָ אֱלֹהֵינוּ, מֶלֶךְ הָעוֹלָם,
בּוֹרֵא מְאוֹרֵי הָאֵשׁ.

Baruch Atah, Adonai Eloheinu, Melech ha'olam, borei m'orei ha'eish.

Praised are You, Adonai our God, Ruler of the universe, who creates the light of the fire.

בָּרוּךְ אַתָּה, יְיָ אֱלֹהֵינוּ, מֶלֶךְ הָעוֹלָם,
הַמַּבְדִּיל בֵּין קֹדֶשׁ לְחֹל, בֵּין אוֹר
לְחֹשֶׁךְ, בֵּין יִשְׂרָאֵל לָעַמִּים, בֵּין
יוֹם הַשְּׁבִיעִי לְשֵׁשֶׁת יְמֵי הַמַּעֲשֶׂה.
בֵּין קְדֻשַּׁת שַׁבָּת לִקְדֻשַּׁת יוֹם טוֹב
הִבְדַּלְתָּ, וְאֶת יוֹם הַשְּׁבִיעִי מִשֵּׁשֶׁת
יְמֵי הַמַּעֲשֶׂה קִדַּשְׁתָּ. הִבְדַּלְתָּ
וְקִדַּשְׁתָּ אֶת עַמְּךָ יִשְׂרָאֵל בִּקְדֻשָּׁתֶךָ.
בָּרוּךְ אַתָּה, יְיָ, הַמַּבְדִּיל בֵּין קֹדֶשׁ
לְקֹדֶשׁ.

Praised are You, Adonai our God, Ruler of the universe, who separates the holy from the ordinary, light from darkness, Israel from other peoples, the seventh day from the six working days, the holiness of Shabbat from the holiness of Yom Tov. You have sanctified Your people Israel with holiness. Praised are You, Adonai, who separates holiness from holiness.

Sheheḥeyanu

We continue by saying (or singing) the Sheheḥeyanu blessing:

Baruch Atah, Adonai Eloheinu, Melech ha'olam, sheheḥeyanu, v'kiy'manu, v'higi'anu lazman hazeh.

בָּרוּךְ אַתָּה, יְיָ אֱלֹהֵינוּ, מֶלֶךְ הָעוֹלָם,
שֶׁהֶחֱיָנוּ וְקִיְּמָנוּ וְהִגִּיעָנוּ לַזְּמַן הַזֶּה.

Praised are You, Adonai our God, Ruler of the universe, who has kept us alive, sustained us, and brought us to this season.

We drink the first cup of wine.

Ur'ḥatz: Washing Our Hands

Washing our hands reminds us that we should be pure as we celebrate the seder. What are some ways that water is important in your life?

We wash our hands at the sink or at the table, using a pitcher and basin. Pour water first over one hand and then over the other. We do not say a blessing at this time.

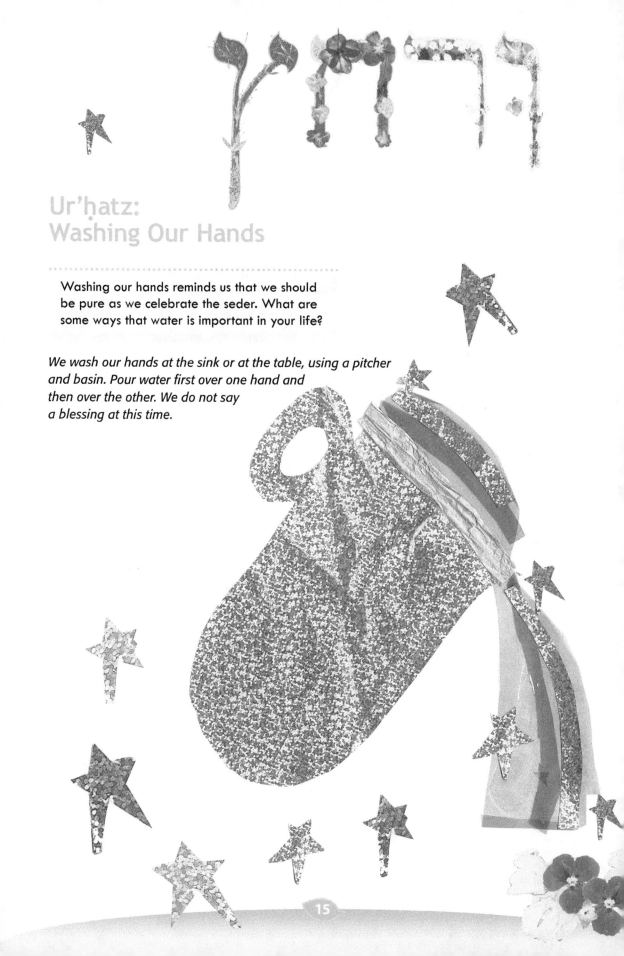

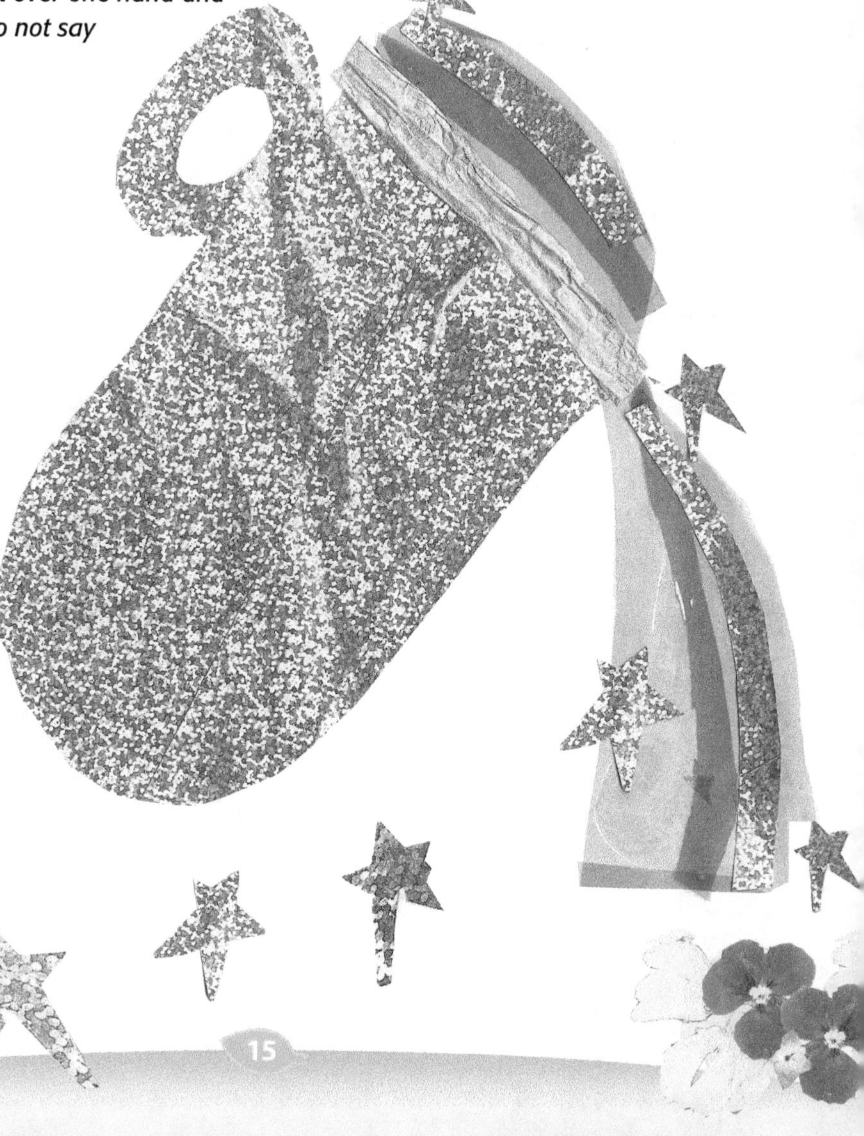

Karpas: Dipping the Greens

We dip a green vegetable (usually parsley or celery) in salt water. Before we eat it, we sing or say:

בָּרוּךְ אַתָּה, יְיָ אֱלֹהֵינוּ, מֶלֶךְ הָעוֹלָם,
בּוֹרֵא פְּרִי הָאֲדָמָה.

Baruch Atah, Adonai Eloheinu, Melech ha'olam, borei p'ri ha'adamah.

Praised are You, Adonai our God, Ruler of the universe, who creates the fruit of the earth.

Now we each eat a piece of the karpas.

The green karpas reminds us that we are celebrating a festival that comes at springtime. The salt water represents the sweat and tears shed by the slaves as they built cities for Pharaoh.

Yaḥatz: Breaking the Middle Matzah

Uncover the plate of matzah and raise it for all to see. Take the middle matzah and break it in two pieces. Put the smaller piece back in the pile. Wrap the larger piece, the afikoman, *and hide it for the children to find after the meal.*

Breaking the matzah can remind us of how God split the sea for the Israelites to cross and escape from Pharaoh and his chariots. We will hide the larger piece of matzah, the afikoman, and later we will share it as dessert after the meal.

Ha laḥma anya di achalu	הָא לַחְמָא עַנְיָא דִּי אֲכָלוּ
Avhatana b'ara d'Mitzrayim.	אַבְהָתָנָא בְּאַרְעָא דְמִצְרָיִם.
Kol dichfin yeitei v'yeichul,	כָּל דִּכְפִין יֵיתֵי וְיֵיכֻל,
Kol ditzrich yeitei v'yifsaḥ.	כָּל דִּצְרִיךְ יֵיתֵי וְיִפְסַח.
Hashata hacha,	הָשַׁתָּא הָכָא,
L'shanah haba'ah b'ara d'Yisrael.	לְשָׁנָה הַבָּאָה בְּאַרְעָא דְיִשְׂרָאֵל.
Hashata avdei,	הָשַׁתָּא עַבְדֵי,
L'shanah haba'ah	לְשָׁנָה הַבָּאָה
B'nei ḥorin.	בְּנֵי חוֹרִין.

This is the bread of poverty that our ancestors ate in the land of Egypt. Let all who are hungry come and eat. Let all who are in need come and celebrate Pesaḥ with us. Now we are here; next year may we be in the Land of Israel. This year we are still slaves; next year may we be truly free.

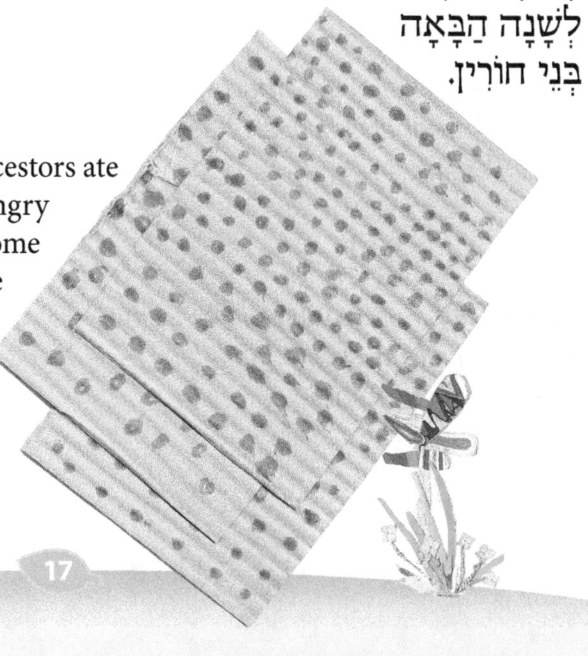

Magid: Telling the Story

Mah Nishtanah

We cover the matzot and pour the second cup of wine. The youngest child reads or sings the Four Questions:

מַה נִּשְׁתַּנָּה הַלַּיְלָה הַזֶּה מִכָּל הַלֵּילוֹת?

Mah nishtanah halailah hazeh mikol haleilot?

שֶׁבְּכָל הַלֵּילוֹת אָנוּ אוֹכְלִין חָמֵץ וּמַצָּה. הַלַּיְלָה הַזֶּה כֻּלּוֹ מַצָּה.

Sheb'chol haleilot anu och'lin ḥameitz umatzah. Halailah hazeh kulo matzah.

שֶׁבְּכָל הַלֵּילוֹת אָנוּ אוֹכְלִין שְׁאָר יְרָקוֹת. הַלַּיְלָה הַזֶּה מָרוֹר.

Sheb'chol haleilot anu och'lin sh'ar y'rakot. Halailah hazeh maror.

שֶׁבְּכָל הַלֵּילוֹת אֵין אָנוּ מַטְבִּילִין אֲפִילוּ פַּעַם אֶחָת. הַלַּיְלָה הַזֶּה שְׁתֵּי פְעָמִים.

Sheb'chol haleilot ein anu matbilin afilu pa'am eḥat. Halailah hazeh sh'tei f'amim.

שֶׁבְּכָל הַלֵּילוֹת אָנוּ אוֹכְלִין בֵּין יוֹשְׁבִין וּבֵין מְסֻבִּין. הַלַּיְלָה הַזֶּה כֻּלָּנוּ מְסֻבִּין.

Sheb'chol haleilot anu och'lin bein yoshvin uvein m'subin. Halailah hazeh kulanu m'subin.

Why is this night different from all other nights?

On all other nights we eat either leavened or unleavened bread.
Tonight, why do we eat only matzah, unleavened bread?

On all other nights we eat any kind of vegetables and herbs.
Tonight, why do we eat *maror* (bitter herbs)?

On all other nights we do not dip herbs even once.
Tonight, why do we dip twice?

On all other nights we eat sitting or leaning.
Tonight, why do we all sit leaning?

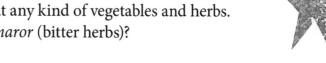

Avadim Hayinu

We were slaves to Pharaoh in Egypt, but God took us out of there with a mighty hand and an outstretched arm. If God had not taken our ancestors out of Egypt, then we, our children, and grandchildren would still be enslaved to a Pharaoh in Egypt. So, even if we were all wise and clever, experienced and learned in Torah, it would still be our duty to tell about the Exodus from Egypt. The more people talk about the story of the Exodus, the more they deserve praise.

עֲבָדִים הָיִינוּ לְפַרְעֹה בְּמִצְרָיִם.
וַיּוֹצִיאֵנוּ יְיָ אֱלֹהֵינוּ מִשָּׁם, בְּיָד
חֲזָקָה וּבִזְרוֹעַ נְטוּיָה. וְאִלּוּ לֹא הוֹצִיא
הַקָּדוֹשׁ בָּרוּךְ הוּא אֶת אֲבוֹתֵינוּ
מִמִּצְרַיִם, הֲרֵי אָנוּ וּבָנֵינוּ וּבְנֵי בָנֵינוּ,
מְשֻׁעְבָּדִים הָיִינוּ לְפַרְעֹה בְּמִצְרָיִם.
וַאֲפִילוּ כֻּלָּנוּ חֲכָמִים, כֻּלָּנוּ נְבוֹנִים,
כֻּלָּנוּ זְקֵנִים, כֻּלָּנוּ יוֹדְעִים אֶת
הַתּוֹרָה, מִצְוָה עָלֵינוּ לְסַפֵּר בִּיצִיאַת
מִצְרָיִם. וְכָל הַמַּרְבֶּה לְסַפֵּר בִּיצִיאַת
מִצְרַיִם, הֲרֵי זֶה מְשֻׁבָּח.

We were once slaves, but now we are free people!

We remember a story from our past. Rabbi Eliezer, Rabbi Joshua, Rabbi Elazar ben Azaryah, Rabbi Akiva, and Rabbi Tarfon were sitting around the seder table in B'nei B'rak. They were so engrossed in talking about the Exodus, that, before they knew it, their students came and said to them, "Rabbis, it is time to say the morning Sh'ma."

This anecdote is meant to emphasize the importance of telling the Passover story, and of learning about our history. Another interpretation says that the elders in this story were actually planning the Bar Kochba Revolt against the Romans (132-135 CE). How can learning about our past help us plan for the future?

Baruch haMakom. Baruch Hu.
Baruch shenatan Torah l'amo Yisrael.
Baruch Hu.

בָּרוּךְ הַמָּקוֹם. בָּרוּךְ הוּא.
בָּרוּךְ שֶׁנָּתַן תּוֹרָה לְעַמּוֹ יִשְׂרָאֵל.
בָּרוּךְ הוּא.

Praised be God. Praised be the Eternal One.
Praised be God who has given the Torah to the people of Israel.
Praised be God.

The Four Children

The Torah tells us to teach our children about the Exodus from Egypt. Four times the Torah repeats, "And you shall tell your child on that day. . . ." From these words we understand that there are four different kinds of children, and to each we must tell the story in a different way.

What does the wise child ask?

"What are the stories, laws and judgments that Adonai our God has commanded?" (Deuteronomy 6:20) To such a child we must explain the laws of Pesaḥ in detail, including that "no afikoman (dessert) may be eaten after the Passover offering." (Mishnah Pesaḥim 10:8)

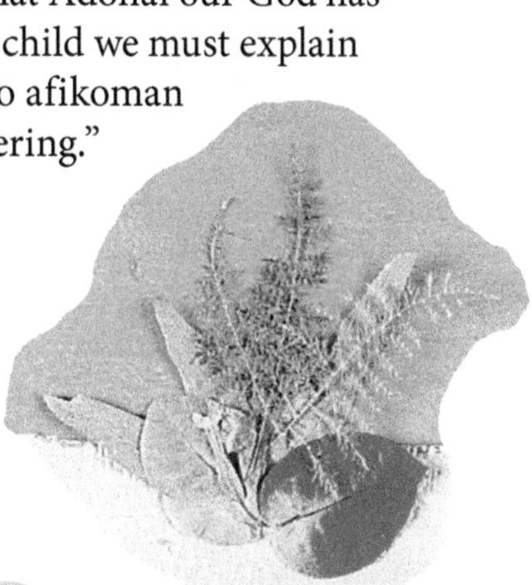

What does the rebellious child ask?

"What does this service mean to you?"(Exodus 12:26) By the words "to you" that child says that this seder service is only for *you*. So we answer the child in the words of the Torah: "This is because of everything God did for me when I came out of Egypt." (Exodus 13:8) For me, not for you; because if you had been there, you would not have been redeemed.

What does the simple child ask?

"What is this?" We answer in the words of the Torah: "With a strong hand God brought us out of Egypt from the house of slavery." (Exodus 13:14)

As for the child who does not know how to ask, you must gently explain, as the Torah teaches: "You shall tell your child on that day: 'This is because of everything God did for me when I came out of Egypt.'" (Exodus 13:8)

The questions asked by the four children represent four ways of approaching the seder experience. From the widely different responses given, we learn the importance of paying attention not only to the words of the questions but also the children's reasons for asking. By considering the motives as well as the words, we are able to give personal responses that will be more meaningful to our listeners. Do you think we each resemble one of the four children, or do we have all of these characteristics at one time or another? Why do you believe this?

V'hi She'amdah

We hold up our wine glasses as we read or sing together:

וְהִיא שֶׁעָמְדָה לַאֲבוֹתֵינוּ וְלָנוּ. שֶׁלֹּא
אֶחָד בִּלְבַד עָמַד עָלֵינוּ לְכַלּוֹתֵנוּ.
אֶלָּא שֶׁבְּכָל דּוֹר וָדוֹר עוֹמְדִים עָלֵינוּ
לְכַלּוֹתֵנוּ. וְהַקָּדוֹשׁ בָּרוּךְ הוּא מַצִּילֵנוּ
מִיָּדָם.

V'hi she'amdah la'avoteinu v'lanu. Shelo eḥad bilvad amad aleinu l'chaloteinu. Ela sheb'chol dor va'dor om'dim aleinu l'chaloteinu. V'ha'Kadosh baruch Hu matzileinu miyadam.

God's promise has given us strength. For not only one enemy has risen against us to destroy us, but in every generation people rise against us. But the Holy One saves us from their hand.

We lower our wine glasses.

The Story of Passover

Our Journey

We now begin the story of our journey from slavery to freedom, from sadness to joy, from oppression to empowerment.

Long before they ever went to Egypt, our ancestors worshipped idols. Abraham, the father of our people, went to the land of Canaan and learned to worship God alone.

In a time of famine our ancestors left Canaan and went down to Mitzrayim, the land of Egypt. There they flourished and became a great nation. Generations passed, and a new Pharaoh came to power who felt no love for the Israelites. When he saw how numerous our ancestors had become, he dealt harshly with them.

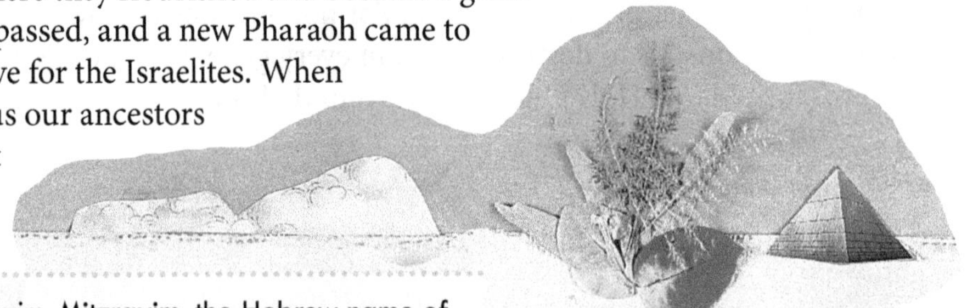

Went down to Mitzrayim. Mitzrayim, the Hebrew name of the land of Egypt, is sometimes used in the seder to refer more generally to a place of restriction. Our ancestors were restricted in their choices because they were slaves. Some interpreters describe Mitzrayim as *m'tzarim,* which means "from the narrows." Pesaḥ is a time when we, celebrating our freedom, can also identify the restricted places in our lives and consider how best to emerge into the wide and hopeful lands beyond.

Slavery in Egypt

Our ancestors became slaves in Mitzrayim, where they spent their days making bricks and building cities for Pharaoh. But still they increased in number until Pharaoh feared that they would rise against him. He cruelly ordered that all the infant boys among the Israelites be killed.

One Israelite woman concealed her son to keep him alive. She placed him in a basket in the Nile and sent the boy's sister, Miriam, to watch over him. Pharaoh's daughter found the boy among the reeds, cared for him, and raised him as her own. She named him Moses, which means "drawn from the water."

Moses grew up in Pharaoh's palace. One day, as an adult, he saw an Egyptian beating an Israelite slave, and he killed the Egyptian. When this crime became known, Moses fled from Mitzrayim to Midian.

At that time the Israelites cried out to the God of their ancestors. When God heard their pleas and saw their suffering, God spoke to Moses through the flames of a bush that seemed to burn without being consumed.

"Let my people go!"

God told Moses to go to Pharaoh and demand that he release the Israelites from slavery. Moses and his brother, Aaron, came before Pharaoh, but Pharaoh refused them, and he made the Israelites work even harder.

Because Pharaoh would not listen, God brought terrible plagues upon the land—blood, frogs, lice, wild beasts, disease, boils, hail, locusts, and darkness. Though his own people suffered from these plagues, Pharaoh's heart remained hardened.

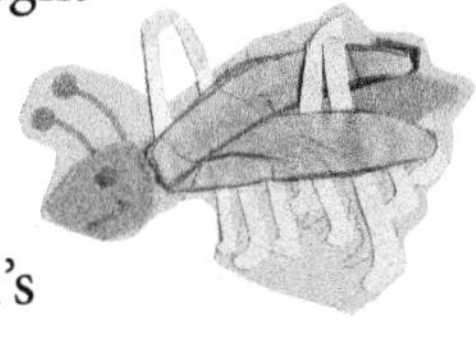

In the last and most terrible plague, every firstborn in the land of Mitzrayim was killed. Only the Israelites were spared. A great wailing rose throughout the land of Mitzrayim, and Pharaoh finally relented. He allowed the Israelites to leave.

Freedom

The Israelites left in a great hurry. When they reached the shore of the Sea of Reeds, Pharaoh changed his mind and sent his armies to pursue them. God caused the Sea of Reeds to split, and the Israelites walked through the dry seabed to safety. Miriam, Moses's sister, led songs of praise to God.

And thus began the Israelites' journey from slavery to the land that God had promised them.

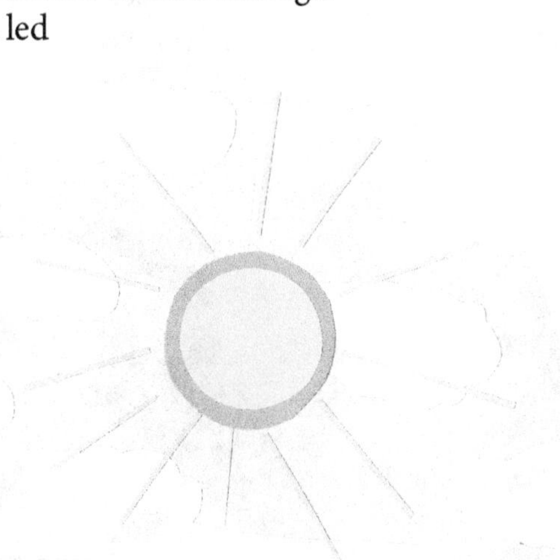

The Ten Plagues

Our rabbis taught: When the Egyptian armies were drowning in the sea, all the angels in heaven began to sing with joy. God silenced them by saying, "My children are drowning and you sing praises?" (Sanhedrin 39b) **So, to this day, we lessen our own joy by removing wine from our cups as we remember those ten terrible plagues.**

Dip a finger or spoon into your wine glass and remove a drop of wine as you recite the name of each plague:

Blood	*Dam*	דָּם
Frogs	*Tz'fardei'a*	צְפַרְדֵּעַ
Lice	*Kinim*	כִּנִּים
Wild beasts	*Arov*	עָרוֹב
Disease	*Dever*	דֶּבֶר
Boils	*Sh'ḥin*	שְׁחִין
Hail	*Barad*	בָּרָד
Locusts	*Arbeh*	אַרְבֶּה
Darkness	*Ḥoshech*	חֹשֶׁךְ
Death of the firstborn	*Makat b'chorot*	מַכַּת בְּכוֹרוֹת

"If your enemy falls, do not celebrate. If your enemy trips, let not your heart rejoice." (Proverbs 24:17)

Dayeinu: It would have been enough!

We sing the following verses of "Dayeinu" together:

Ilu hotzi'anu mi'Mitzrayim, dayeinu.
Ilu natan lanu et haShabbat, dayeinu.
Ilu natan lanu et haTorah, dayeinu.
Ilu hichnisanu l'Eretz Yisrael, dayeinu.

אִלּוּ הוֹצִיאָנוּ מִמִּצְרַיִם, דַּיֵּנוּ.
אִלּוּ נָתַן לָנוּ אֶת הַשַּׁבָּת, דַּיֵּנוּ.
אִלּוּ נָתַן לָנוּ אֶת הַתּוֹרָה, דַּיֵּנוּ.
אִלּוּ הִכְנִיסָנוּ לְאֶרֶץ יִשְׂרָאֵל, דַּיֵּנוּ.

The leader recites each verse, and everyone responds "dayeinu."

God has given us many gifts, but even one of them would have been enough!

כַּמָּה מַעֲלוֹת טוֹבוֹת לַמָּקוֹם עָלֵינוּ.

If God had only brought us out of Egypt and had not divided the sea for us, *dayeinu*!

אִלּוּ הוֹצִיאָנוּ מִמִּצְרַיִם,
וְלֹא קָרַע לָנוּ אֶת הַיָּם, דַּיֵּנוּ.

Had God divided the sea for us and not led us through onto dry land, *dayeinu*!

אִלּוּ קָרַע לָנוּ אֶת הַיָּם,
וְלֹא הֶעֱבִירָנוּ בְתוֹכוֹ בֶּחָרָבָה, דַּיֵּנוּ.

Had God led us through onto dry land and not watched over us in the desert for forty years, *dayeinu*!

אִלּוּ הֶעֱבִירָנוּ בְתוֹכוֹ בֶּחָרָבָה,
וְלֹא סִפֵּק צָרְכֵּנוּ בַּמִּדְבָּר אַרְבָּעִים
שָׁנָה, דַּיֵּנוּ.

Had God watched over us in the desert for forty years and not fed us with *manna*, *dayeinu*!

אִלּוּ סִפֵּק צָרְכֵּנוּ בַּמִּדְבָּר אַרְבָּעִים שָׁנָה,
וְלֹא הֶאֱכִילָנוּ אֶת הַמָּן, דַּיֵּנוּ.

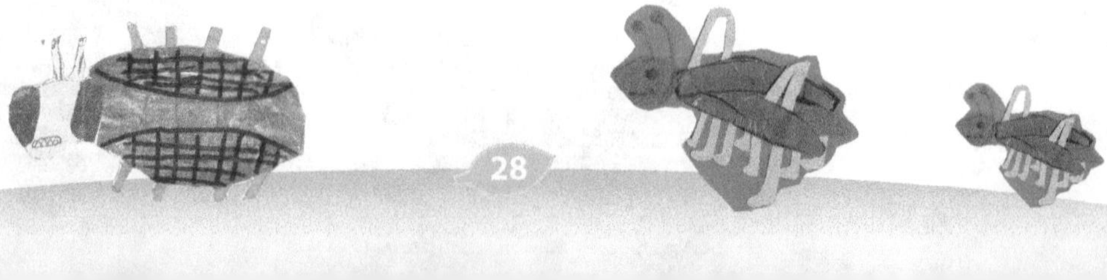

Had God fed us with manna
and not given us Shabbat, *dayeinu*!

אִלּוּ הֶאֱכִילָנוּ אֶת הַמָּן,
וְלֹא נָתַן לָנוּ אֶת הַשַּׁבָּת, דַּיֵּנוּ.

Had God given us Shabbat
and not brought us to Mount Sinai, *dayeinu*!

אִלּוּ נָתַן לָנוּ אֶת הַשַּׁבָּת,
וְלֹא קֵרְבָנוּ לִפְנֵי הַר סִינַי, דַּיֵּנוּ.

Had God brought us to Mount Sinai
and not given us the Torah, *dayeinu*!

אִלּוּ קֵרְבָנוּ לִפְנֵי הַר סִינַי,
וְלֹא נָתַן לָנוּ אֶת הַתּוֹרָה, דַּיֵּנוּ.

Had God given us the Torah
and not brought us to the land of
Israel, *dayeinu*!

אִלּוּ נָתַן לָנוּ אֶת הַתּוֹרָה,
וְלֹא הִכְנִיסָנוּ לְאֶרֶץ יִשְׂרָאֵל, דַּיֵּנוּ.

Had God brought us to the land of Israel
and not built the Temple for us, *dayeinu*!

אִלּוּ הִכְנִיסָנוּ לְאֶרֶץ יִשְׂרָאֵל, וְלֹא
בָנָה לָנוּ אֶת בֵּית הַבְּחִירָה, דַּיֵּנוּ.

What are some things in your own life for which you could say "*dayeinu*"?

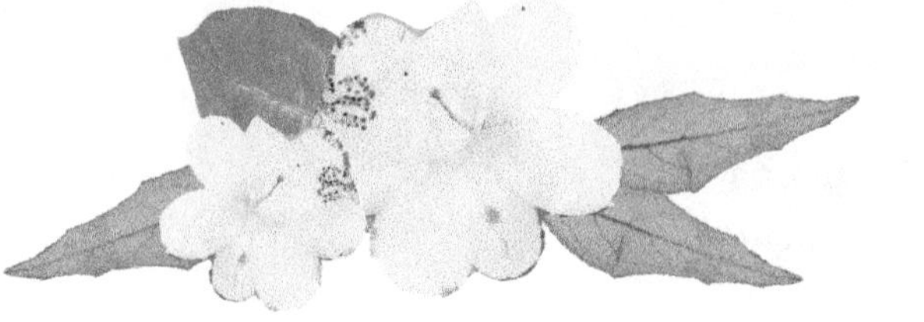

When we finish "Dayeinu," we review all of God's blessings:

עַל אַחַת כַּמָּה וְכַמָּה טוֹבָה כְפוּלָה
וּמְכֻפֶּלֶת לַמָּקוֹם עָלֵינוּ.

How much more so, then, should we give thanks for the many good things God has done for us!

שֶׁהוֹצִיאָנוּ מִמִּצְרַיִם, וְעָשָׂה בָהֶם
שְׁפָטִים, וְעָשָׂה בֵאלֹהֵיהֶם, וְהָרַג
אֶת בְּכוֹרֵיהֶם, וְנָתַן לָנוּ אֶת מָמוֹנָם,
וְקָרַע לָנוּ אֶת הַיָּם, וְהֶעֱבִירָנוּ
בְתוֹכוֹ בֶּחָרָבָה, וְשִׁקַּע צָרֵינוּ בְּתוֹכוֹ,
וְסִפֵּק צָרְכֵּנוּ בַּמִּדְבָּר אַרְבָּעִים שָׁנָה,
וְהֶאֱכִילָנוּ אֶת הַמָּן, וְנָתַן לָנוּ אֶת
הַשַּׁבָּת, וְקֵרְבָנוּ לִפְנֵי הַר סִינַי, וְנָתַן
לָנוּ אֶת הַתּוֹרָה, וְהִכְנִיסָנוּ לְאֶרֶץ
יִשְׂרָאֵל, וּבָנָה לָנוּ אֶת בֵּית הַבְּחִירָה.

God brought us out of Egypt, divided the sea for us, led us through onto dry land, watched over us in the desert for forty years, fed us with manna, gave us Shabbat, brought us to Mount Sinai, gave us the Torah, brought us to the land of Israel, and built the Temple for us.

Pesaḥ, Matzah, Maror

Rabbi Gamaliel used to say: If on Passover you do not explain these three things, you have not fulfilled the purpose of the seder: *Pesaḥ*, the Passover offering; *Matzah*, the unleavened bread; and *Maror*, the bitter herbs.

Hold up the roasted bone. (Vegetarians sometimes use a beet instead.)

פֶּסַח שֶׁהָיוּ אֲבוֹתֵינוּ אוֹכְלִים בִּזְמַן שֶׁבֵּית הַמִּקְדָּשׁ הָיָה קַיָּם, עַל שׁוּם מָה?

What is the meaning of Pesaḥ?

The roasted bone (or beet) reminds us of the Passover sacrifice that our ancestors offered in the Temple in Jerusalem. As it is written: "You shall say: It is the Passover offering for Adonai, who passed over the houses of the children of Israel in Mitzrayim and punished the Egyptians." (Exodus 12:27)

Hold up the matzah.

מַצָּה זוֹ שֶׁאָנוּ אוֹכְלִים, עַל שׁוּם מָה?

Why do we eat this matzah?

Because the Torah tells us, "They baked the dough that they had brought out of Mitzrayim into unleavened bread; for they were driven out of Mitzrayim and could not delay, nor had they prepared any food for their journey." (Exodus 12:39)

Hold up the dish of maror.

Why do we eat this bitter maror?

מָרוֹר זֶה שֶׁאָנוּ אוֹכְלִים, עַל שׁוּם מָה?

It is because the Egyptians made the lives of our ancestors miserable in Mitzrayim, as it is written: "They made life bitter for them with hard work, with clay and bricks, and with all kinds of work in the field; whatever work they did was backbreaking." (Exodus 1:14)

B'chol Dor Va'dor

In every generation it is our duty to think of ourselves as though we personally had come out of Egypt, as it is written: "You shall tell your children on that day: 'This is because of what God did for me when I came out of Mitzrayim.'" (Exodus 13:8)

בְּכָל דּוֹר וָדוֹר חַיָּב אָדָם לִרְאוֹת
אֶת עַצְמוֹ כְּאִלּוּ הוּא יָצָא מִמִּצְרָיִם,
שֶׁנֶּאֱמַר: וְהִגַּדְתָּ לְבִנְךָ בַּיּוֹם הַהוּא
לֵאמֹר בַּעֲבוּר זֶה עָשָׂה יְיָ לִי בְּצֵאתִי
מִמִּצְרָיִם.

We raise our cups of wine and read together:

Therefore let us rejoice at the wonder of our deliverance.
God took us from slavery to freedom,
From sadness to joy,
From sorrow to singing,
From darkness to a great light,
From slavery to redemption.
So let us sing a new song before God!
Halleluyah!

Psalm 113

הַלְלוּיָהּ, הַלְלוּ עַבְדֵי יְיָ, הַלְלוּ אֶת
שֵׁם יְיָ. יְהִי שֵׁם יְיָ מְבֹרָךְ מֵעַתָּה וְעַד
עוֹלָם.

Halleluyah! Praise, you servants of Adonai, praise the name of God. Praised be the name of God from this time forth and forever.

From the rising of the sun to its setting, God's name is to be praised. High above all nations is Adonai; above the heavens is God's glory. Who is like Adonai our God, who, though enthroned on high, looks down upon heaven and earth? God raises the poor out of the dust and lifts the needy out of the dust, to seat them with the highest of God's people. God turns the barren woman into a happy mother of children. Halleluyah!

Psalm 114

בְּצֵאת יִשְׂרָאֵל מִמִּצְרָיִם, בֵּית יַעֲקֹב
מֵעַם לֹעֵז. הָיְתָה יְהוּדָה לְקָדְשׁוֹ,
יִשְׂרָאֵל מַמְשְׁלוֹתָיו. הַיָּם רָאָה וַיָּנֹס,
הַיַּרְדֵּן יִסֹּב לְאָחוֹר.

B'tzeit Yisrael miMitzrayim, beit Ya'akov mei'am lo'eiz. Haitah Y'hudah l'kodsho, Yisrael mamsh'lotav. Hayam ra'ah vayanos, haYardein yisov l'aḥor.

When Israel went out of Mitzrayim, Jacob's household from a people of foreign speech, Judah became God's sanctuary, Israel God's kingdom. The sea saw it and fled; the Jordan turned backward. The mountains skipped like rams, and the hills like lambs. Why is it, O sea, that you flee? Why, O Jordan, do you turn backward? You mountains, why do you skip like rams? You hills, why do you skip like lambs? O earth, tremble at God's presence, at the presence of the God of Jacob, who turns the rock into a pool of water, the flint into a flowing spring.

The Second Cup of Wine

We raise the second cup of wine and read together God's second promise to our ancestors and to us:

וְהִצַּלְתִּי אֶתְכֶם מֵעֲבֹדָתָם.

"I will deliver you from slavery."
(Exodus 6:6)

בָּרוּךְ אַתָּה, יְיָ אֱלֹהֵינוּ, מֶלֶךְ הָעוֹלָם, אֲשֶׁר גְּאָלָנוּ וְגָאַל אֶת אֲבוֹתֵינוּ מִמִּצְרַיִם, וְהִגִּיעָנוּ לַלַּיְלָה הַזֶּה, לֶאֱכָל בּוֹ מַצָּה וּמָרוֹר. כֵּן יְיָ אֱלֹהֵינוּ וֵאלֹהֵי אֲבוֹתֵינוּ יַגִּיעֵנוּ לְמוֹעֲדִים וְלִרְגָלִים אֲחֵרִים, הַבָּאִים לִקְרָאתֵנוּ לְשָׁלוֹם, שְׂמֵחִים בְּבִנְיַן עִירֶךָ, וְשָׂשִׂים בַּעֲבוֹדָתֶךָ, וְנוֹדֶה לְּךָ שִׁיר חָדָשׁ עַל גְּאֻלָּתֵנוּ, וְעַל פְּדוּת נַפְשֵׁנוּ.

Praised are You, Adonai our God, Ruler of the universe, who has redeemed us and our ancestors from Mitzrayim and enabled us to reach this night that we may eat matzah and maror. Our God and God of our ancestors, may we reach all the holidays and festivals in peace, rejoicing in the rebuilding of Zion and joyful at this service. There we shall sing a new song of praise to You for our rescue and for our freedom.

Baruch Atah, Adonai, ga'al Yisrael.

בָּרוּךְ אַתָּה, יְיָ, גָּאַל יִשְׂרָאֵל.

Praised are You, Adonai, who has redeemed Israel.

We sing the blessing for the second cup of wine:

Baruch Atah, Adonai Eloheinu, Melech ha'olam, borei p'ri hagafen.

בָּרוּךְ אַתָּה, יְיָ אֱלֹהֵינוּ, מֶלֶךְ הָעוֹלָם, בּוֹרֵא פְּרִי הַגָּפֶן.

Praised are You, Adonai our God, Ruler of the universe, who creates the fruit of the vine.

We drink the second cup of wine.

רחצה

Roḥtzah: Washing Our Hands

We pause here for the ritual hand washing that precedes a meal. After the hand washing, we recite the following blessing:

בָּרוּךְ אַתָּה, יְיָ אֱלֹהֵינוּ, מֶלֶךְ הָעוֹלָם,
אֲשֶׁר קִדְּשָׁנוּ בְּמִצְוֹתָיו וְצִוָּנוּ עַל
נְטִילַת יָדָיִם.

Baruch Atah, Adonai Eloheinu, Melech ha'olam, asher kid'shanu b'mitzvotav v'tzivanu al n'tilat yadayim.

Praised are You, Adonai our God, Ruler of the universe, who makes us holy with commandments, and commands us to wash our hands.

מוציא מצה

Motzi Matzah: Blessings for the Matzah

We uncover the plate of matzah and raise it for all to see. We recite the following two blessings over the matzah. The first is a blessing for eating food; the second, a blessing for the special mitzvah of eating matzah on a seder night.

בָּרוּךְ אַתָּה, יְיָ אֱלֹהֵינוּ, מֶלֶךְ הָעוֹלָם,
הַמּוֹצִיא לֶחֶם מִן הָאָרֶץ.

Baruch Atah, Adonai Eloheinu, Melech ha'olam, hamotzi leḥem min ha'aretz.

Praised are You, Adonai our God, Ruler of the universe, who brings bread from the earth.

We recite the second blessing while holding up the top and middle matzah:

בָּרוּךְ אַתָּה, יְיָ אֱלֹהֵינוּ, מֶלֶךְ הָעוֹלָם,
אֲשֶׁר קִדְּשָׁנוּ בְּמִצְוֹתָיו וְצִוָּנוּ עַל
אֲכִילַת מַצָּה.

Baruch Atah, Adonai Eloheinu, Melech ha'olam, asher kid'shanu b'mitzvotav v'tzivanu al achilat matzah.

Praised are You, Adonai our God, Ruler of the universe, who makes us holy with commandments, and commands us to eat matzah.

We each eat a piece from the top or middle matzah.

Maror:
The Bitter Herbs

We dip the bitter herbs in ḥaroset and recite the blessing:

בָּרוּךְ אַתָּה, יְיָ אֱלֹהֵינוּ, מֶלֶךְ הָעוֹלָם,
אֲשֶׁר קִדְּשָׁנוּ בְּמִצְוֹתָיו וְצִוָּנוּ עַל
אֲכִילַת מָרוֹר.

Baruch Atah, Adonai Eloheinu, Melech ha'olam, asher kid'shanu b'mitzvotav v'tzivanu al achilat maror.

Praised are You, Adonai our God, Ruler of the universe, who makes us holy with commandments, and commands us to eat maror.

We eat the bitter herbs.

The ḥaroset reminds us of the mortar and bricks used for the building of Pharaoh's cities in Egypt. Dipping bitter maror in sweet ḥaroset can remind us of the hope that enabled our ancestors to withstand the bitterness of slavery. Describe a time when hopeful thoughts helped you to deal with something sad or unpleasant.

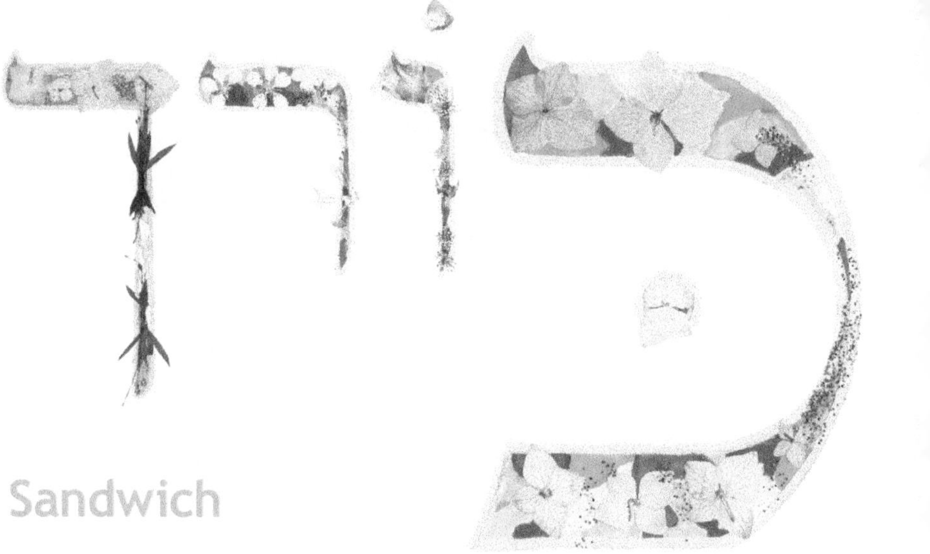

Koreich: The Hillel Sandwich

We combine a second serving of maror (or ḥazeret, which may be romaine lettuce or another bitter herb) with a portion of the bottom matzah to make the Hillel sandwich. Some people add ḥaroset, as well.

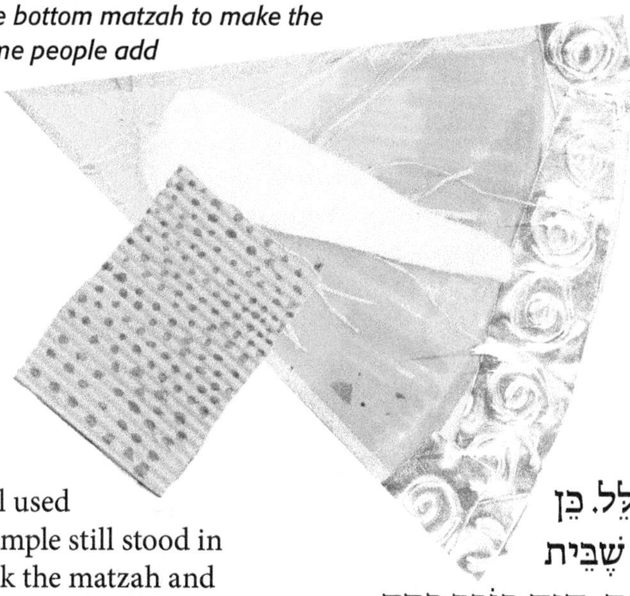

We read together:

זֵכֶר לְמִקְדָּשׁ כְּהִלֵּל. כֵּן
עָשָׂה הִלֵּל בִּזְמַן שֶׁבֵּית
הַמִּקְדָּשׁ הָיָה קַיָּם. הָיָה כּוֹרֵךְ פֶּסַח
מַצָּה וּמָרוֹר וְאוֹכֵל בְּיַחַד, לְקַיֵּם מַה
שֶּׁנֶּאֱמַר: עַל מַצּוֹת וּמְרוֹרִים יֹאכְלֻהוּ.

This is what Hillel used to do when the Temple still stood in Jerusalem. He took the matzah and maror and ate them together with the Pesaḥ offering, to fulfill the words of the Torah: "They shall eat it with unleavened bread and bitter herbs." (Numbers 9:11)

The great teacher Hillel lived in Jerusalem during the first century BCE. His teachings had a profound influence on Jewish thought, and continue to influence Judaism today.

שלחן עורך

Shulḥan Oreich:
The Meal

The festival meal is a mitzvah and part of the seder service. We eat with joy and reverence to fulfill the mitzvah.

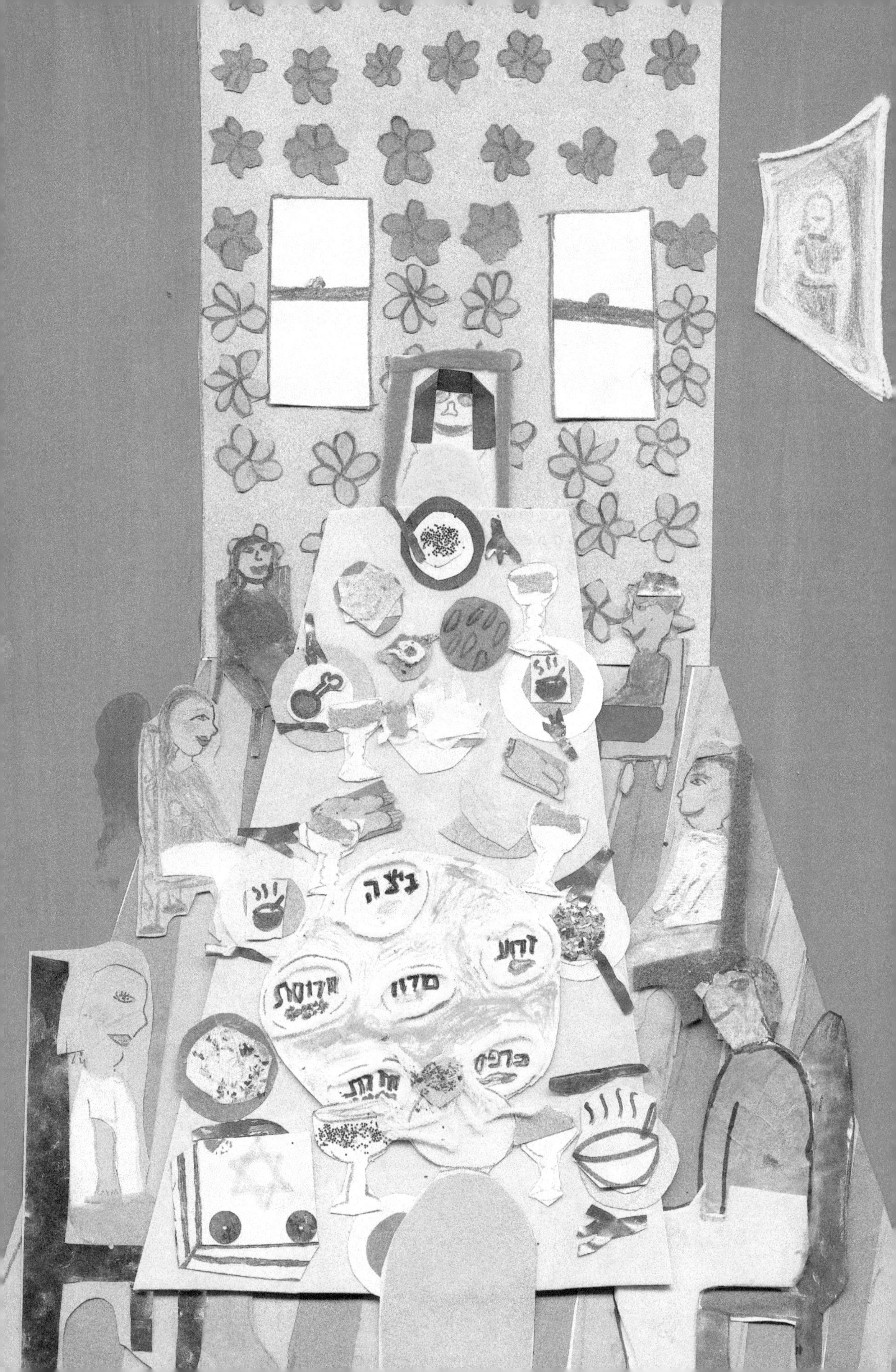
ביצה
זרוע
חרוסת
מרור
כרפס

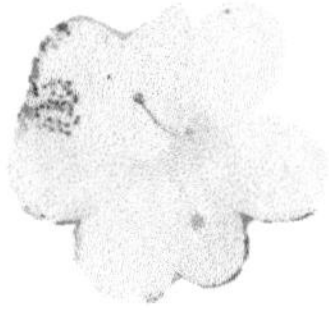

Tzafun: The Afikoman

After the meal, the leader gives a prize to whomever finds the hidden matzah, and distributes a piece of afikoman to each of the seder participants. Only after eating the afikoman can we continue our seder.

Bareich:
Blessing after the Meal

We now fill the third cup and sing Birkat Hamazon, the blessing after the meal. The following is a short version of the blessing:

בָּרוּךְ אַתָּה, יְיָ אֱלֹהֵינוּ, מֶלֶךְ הָעוֹלָם,
הַזָּן אֶת הָעוֹלָם כֻּלּוֹ בְּטוּבוֹ בְּחֵן
בְּחֶסֶד וּבְרַחֲמִים. הוּא נוֹתֵן לֶחֶם לְכָל
בָּשָׂר כִּי לְעוֹלָם חַסְדּוֹ. וּבְטוּבוֹ הַגָּדוֹל
תָּמִיד לֹא חָסַר לָנוּ, וְאַל יֶחְסַר לָנוּ
מָזוֹן לְעוֹלָם וָעֶד בַּעֲבוּר שְׁמוֹ הַגָּדוֹל,
כִּי הוּא אֵל זָן וּמְפַרְנֵס לַכֹּל וּמֵטִיב
לַכֹּל, וּמֵכִין מָזוֹן לְכָל בְּרִיּוֹתָיו אֲשֶׁר
בָּרָא. בָּרוּךְ אַתָּה, יְיָ, הַזָּן אֶת הַכֹּל.

Baruch Atah, Adonai Eloheinu, Melech ha'olam, hazan et ha'olam kulo b'tuvo b'ḥein b'ḥesed uv'raḥamim. Hu notein leḥem l'chol basar ki l'olam ḥasdo. Uv'tuvo hagadol tamid lo ḥasar lanu, v'al yeḥsar lanu mazon l'olam va'ed ba'avur sh'mo hagadol, ki hu El zan um'farneis lakol umeitiv lakol, umeichin mazon l'chol b'riyotav asher bara. Baruch Atah, Adonai, hazan et hakol.

Praised are You, Adonai our God, Ruler of the universe, who nourishes the whole world with goodness, grace, kindness, and mercy. You give food to all creatures, for Your kindness endures forever. Through this great goodness we have never been in want; may we never be in need of food for the sake of God's great name. We give thanks to God who nourishes and sustains all, does good to all, and provides food for all creation. Praised are You, Adonai, who nourishes all.

The Third Cup of Wine

We raise the third cup of wine and read together God's third promise to our ancestors and to us:

"I will redeem you with an outstretched arm." (Exodus 6:6)

וְגָאַלְתִּי אֶתְכֶם בִּזְרוֹעַ נְטוּיָה.

We sing the blessing over the third cup of wine.

Baruch Atah, Adonai Eloheinu, Melech ha'olam, borei p'ri hagafen.

בָּרוּךְ אַתָּה, יְיָ אֱלֹהֵינוּ, מֶלֶךְ הָעוֹלָם,
בּוֹרֵא פְּרִי הַגָּפֶן.

Praised are you, Adonai our God, Ruler of the universe, who creates the fruit of the vine.

We drink the third cup of wine.

Elijah's Cup

We pour a fourth cup of wine for each person present, and an extra cup in honor of the Prophet Elijah.

Tradition teaches us that the Prophet Elijah is the long-expected messenger who will tell us when the sovereignty of God is about to arrive, ushering in peace and perfection. We can fill Elijah's Cup by inviting participants to pour a little wine or grape juice from their cup into Elijah's. This reminds us that we all must do our part to create a better world and bring about our redemption.

We open the door to welcome Elijah, and everyone sings:

אֵלִיָּהוּ הַנָּבִיא,
אֵלִיָּהוּ הַתִּשְׁבִּי,
אֵלִיָּהוּ, אֵלִיָּהוּ,
אֵלִיָּהוּ הַגִּלְעָדִי,
בִּמְהֵרָה בְיָמֵינוּ
יָבֹא אֵלֵינוּ
עִם מָשִׁיחַ בֶּן דָּוִד.

Eliyahu hanavi,
Eliyahu haTishbi
Eliyahu, Eliyahu, Eliyahu haGiladi,
Bimheirah v'yameinu yavo eileinu
Im Mashiaḥ ben David.

Elijah the prophet, Elijah the Tishbite,
Elijah, Elijah, Elijah from Gilad,
Quickly in our days he will come to us,
with the Messiah, son of David.

Miriam's Cup
We fill a cup with water in honor of Miriam's role in the Exodus. Miriam guarded her brother Moses along the banks of the Nile and led the women in song beside the Sea of Reeds. Tradition teaches that Miriam's Well miraculously followed the Israelites through the desert, providing fresh water until the day Miriam died.

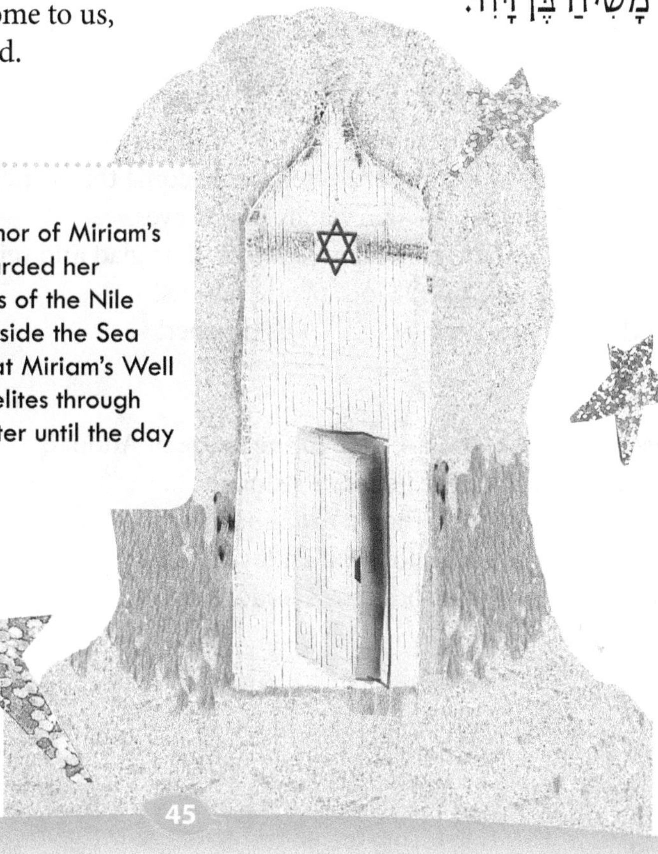

Hallel:
Psalms of Praise

Psalm 117

Give thanks to God, all you nations;
Praise God, all you peoples!
For God's kindness overwhelms us, and the truth of Adonai is forever.
Halleluyah!

From Psalm 118

Give thanks to God, who is good; God's kindness endures forever.
Let Israel say: God's kindness endures forever.
Let the house of Aaron say: God's kindness endures forever.
Let those who revere Adonai say: God's kindness endures forever.

I thank You for You have answered me and have become my salvation.
The stone that the builders rejected has become the cornerstone.
This is God's doing, it is marvelous in our eyes.
This is the day that God has made; we will be glad and rejoice in it.
O God, please save us! O God, please save us!
O God, let us prosper! O God, let us prosper!

Praised are those who are here in the name of Adonai;
We praise you from the house of Adonai. . . .
You are my God, and I thank You; You are my God, and I glorify You.
Give thanks to Adonai, for God endures forever;
And God's loving-kindness endures forever.

Nishmat

The soul of every living being shall praise Your name, Adonai our God,
And the spirit of all people shall glorify and exalt You, our Ruler.
Beyond eternity to eternity, you are God. We have no Sovereign but You—
God of the first and of the last, God of all creatures and of all generations.

If only our mouths filled with song as the sea,
and our tongues with joy as the endless waves;

Our lips full of praise as the heavens are wide,
and our eyes shining like the sun and the moon;

If only our hands spread out in prayer as eagles' wings
and our feet as swift as the deer—

We would still be unable to thank You and praise Your name,
our God and God of our people,

For a single one of the thousands and tens of thousands of good things that
You have given to our ancestors and to us.

You freed us from Mitzrayim and rescued us from a life of slavery.

Therefore, O God, limbs and tongue and heart and
mind join now to give You thanks.

To You, every mouth shall offer thanks, every tongue
shall vow loyalty, every knee shall bend, and all who
stand shall praise You, as it is written: "All my bones shall
say: 'O God, who is like You?'" (Psalm 35:10)

Who is equal to You? Who can be compared to You?

As David sang, "Praise Adonai, O my soul, and let all
my being praise God's holy name." (Psalm 103:1)

The Fourth Cup of Wine

We raise the fourth cup of wine and read together God's fourth promise to our ancestors and to us:

"I will take you to be my people, and I will be your God." (Exodus 6:7)

וְלָקַחְתִּי אֶתְכֶם לִי לְעָם וְהָיִיתִי לָכֶם לֵאלֹהִים.

We sing the blessing together:

Baruch Atah, Adonai Eloheinu, Melech ha'olam, borei p'ri hagafen.

בָּרוּךְ אַתָּה, יְיָ אֱלֹהֵינוּ, מֶלֶךְ הָעוֹלָם, בּוֹרֵא פְּרִי הַגָּפֶן.

Praised are You, Adonai our God, Ruler of the universe, who creates the fruit of the vine.

We drink the fourth cup of wine.

Praised are You, Adonai our God, Ruler of the universe, for the vine and its fruit, and for the produce of the field, and for the beautiful and spacious land that You gave to our people to eat of its fruit and enjoy its goodness.

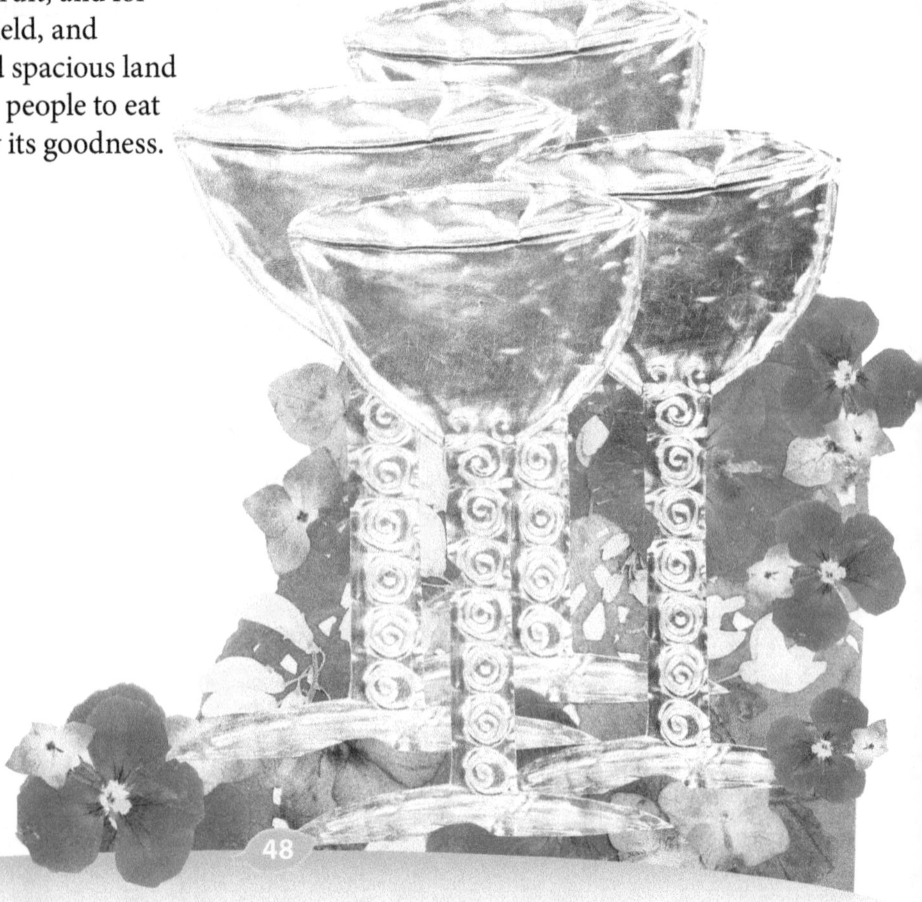

נרצה

Nirtzah: Concluding our Seder

We read together:

The seder service now concludes,
Complete in all its laws and customs.
May God who broke Pharaoh's power
Bring peace and freedom to every land.
O Pure One, who dwells above,
Establish us as a countless people.
Speedily guide us as a people redeemed
To the land of Zion with song.

חֲסַל סִדּוּר פֶּסַח כְּהִלְכָתוֹ,
כְּכָל מִשְׁפָּטוֹ וְחֻקָּתוֹ.
כַּאֲשֶׁר זָכִינוּ לְסַדֵּר אוֹתוֹ,
כֵּן נִזְכֶּה לַעֲשׂוֹתוֹ.
זָךְ שׁוֹכֵן מְעוֹנָה,
קוֹמֵם קְהַל עֲדַת מִי מָנָה.
בְּקָרוֹב נַהֵל נִטְעֵי כַנָּה,
פְּדוּיִם לְצִיּוֹן בְּרִנָּה.

לְשָׁנָה
הַבָּאָה
בִּירוּשָׁלָיִם.

L'shanah
haba'ah
biY'rushalayim!

Next year in Jerusalem!

Shirim: Songs for Pesaḥ

Ki Lo Na'eh

Ki lo na'eh, ki lo ya'eh.
Adir bimluchah, baḥur kahalachah,
g'dudav yomru lo:
L'cha ul'cha, l'cha ki l'cha, l'cha af l'cha,
l'cha Adonai hamamlachah.
Ki lo na'eh, ki lo ya'eh.

כִּי לוֹ נָאֶה, כִּי לוֹ יָאֶה.
אַדִּיר בִּמְלוּכָה, בָּחוּר כַּהֲלָכָה,
גְּדוּדָיו יֹאמְרוּ לוֹ:
לְךָ וּלְךָ, לְךָ כִּי לְךָ, לְךָ אַף לְךָ,
לְךָ יְיָ הַמַּמְלָכָה.
כִּי לוֹ נָאֶה, כִּי לוֹ יָאֶה.

Dagul bimluchah, hadur kahalachah,
vatikav yomru lo:
L'cha ul'cha, l'cha ki l'cha, l'cha af l'cha,
l'cha Adonai hamamlachah.
Ki lo na'eh, ki lo ya'eh.

דָּגוּל בִּמְלוּכָה, הָדוּר כַּהֲלָכָה,
וָתִיקָיו יֹאמְרוּ לוֹ:
לְךָ וּלְךָ, לְךָ כִּי לְךָ, לְךָ אַף לְךָ,
לְךָ יְיָ הַמַּמְלָכָה.
כִּי לוֹ נָאֶה, כִּי לוֹ יָאֶה.

זַכַּאי בִּמְלוּכָה, חָסִין כַּהֲלָכָה,
טַפְסְרָיו יֹאמְרוּ לוֹ:
לְךָ וּלְךָ, לְךָ כִּי לְךָ, לְךָ אַף לְךָ,
לְךָ יְיָ הַמַּמְלָכָה.
כִּי לוֹ נָאֶה, כִּי לוֹ יָאֶה.

Zakai bimluchah, ḥasin kahalachah,
tafs'rav yomru lo:
L'cha ul'cha, l'cha ki l'cha, l'cha af l'cha,
l'cha Adonai hamamlachah.
Ki lo na'eh, ki lo ya'eh.

יָחִיד בִּמְלוּכָה, כַּבִּיר כַּהֲלָכָה,
לִמּוּדָיו יֹאמְרוּ לוֹ:
לְךָ וּלְךָ, לְךָ כִּי לְךָ, לְךָ אַף לְךָ,
לְךָ יְיָ הַמַּמְלָכָה.
כִּי לוֹ נָאֶה, כִּי לוֹ יָאֶה.

Yaḥid bimluchah, kabir kahalachah,
limudav yomru lo:
L'cha ul'cha, l'cha ki l'cha, l'cha af l'cha,
l'cha Adonai hamamlachah.
Ki lo na'eh, ki lo ya'eh.

Beautiful praises are God's due.

With royal power, truly chosen, God's hosts sing:
"To You, only You, O God, is sovereignty." Beautiful praises are God's due.

With royal fame, truly glorious, God's faithful sing:
"To You, only You, O God, is sovereignty." Beautiful praises are God's due.

With royal entitlement, truly protected, God's angels sing:
"To You, only You, O God, is sovereignty." Beautiful praises are God's due.

Unique in sovereignty, truly strong, God's disciples sing:
"To You, only You, O God, is sovereignty." Beautiful praises are God's due.

Adir Hu

Adir Hu, adir Hu,
Yivneh veito b'karov,
Bimheirah bimheirah, b'yameinu b'karov.
El b'neih, El b'neih, b'neih veit'cha
b'karov.

אַדִּיר הוּא, אַדִּיר הוּא,
יִבְנֶה בֵיתוֹ בְּקָרוֹב,
בִּמְהֵרָה בִּמְהֵרָה, בְּיָמֵינוּ בְּקָרוֹב.
אֵל בְּנֵה, אֵל בְּנֵה, בְּנֵה בֵיתְךָ בְּקָרוֹב.

Baḥur Hu, gadol Hu, dagul Hu,
Yivneh veito b'karov,
Bimheirah bimheirah, b'yameinu b'karov.
El b'neih, El b'neih, b'neih veit'cha
b'karov.

בָּחוּר הוּא, גָּדוֹל הוּא, דָּגוּל הוּא,
יִבְנֶה בֵיתוֹ בְּקָרוֹב,
בִּמְהֵרָה בִּמְהֵרָה, בְּיָמֵינוּ בְּקָרוֹב.
אֵל בְּנֵה, אֵל בְּנֵה, בְּנֵה בֵיתְךָ בְּקָרוֹב.

Hadur Hu, vatik Hu, zakai Hu,
Ḥasid Hu, tahor Hu, yaḥid Hu,
Kabir Hu, lamud Hu, melech Hu,
Nora Hu, sagiv Hu, izuz Hu,
Podeh Hu, tzadik Hu, kadosh Hu,
Raḥum Hu, Shadai Hu, takif Hu,

הָדוּר הוּא, וָתִיק הוּא, זַכַּאי הוּא,
חָסִיד הוּא, טָהוֹר הוּא, יָחִיד הוּא,
כַּבִּיר הוּא, לָמוּד הוּא, מֶלֶךְ הוּא,
נוֹרָא הוּא, סַגִּיב הוּא, עִזּוּז הוּא,
פּוֹדֶה הוּא, צַדִּיק הוּא, קָדוֹשׁ הוּא,
רַחוּם הוּא, שַׁדַּי הוּא, תַּקִּיף הוּא,

Yivneh veito b'karov,
Bimheirah bimheirah, b'yameinu b'karov.
El b'neih, El b'neih, b'neih veit'cha
b'karov.

יִבְנֶה בֵיתוֹ בְּקָרוֹב,
בִּמְהֵרָה בִּמְהֵרָה, בְּיָמֵינוּ בְּקָרוֹב.
אֵל בְּנֵה, אֵל בְּנֵה, בְּנֵה בֵיתְךָ בְּקָרוֹב.

The verses of this song begin with different synonyms for "glorious." In Hebrew, these synonyms start with all the letters of the Hebrew alphabet, in order.

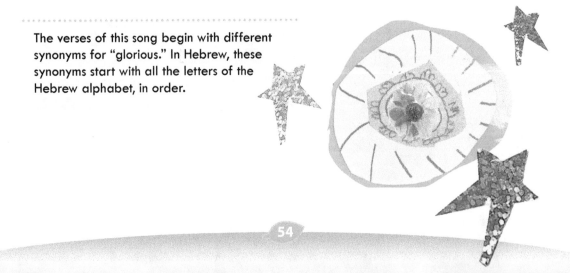

Glorious is God, glorious is God,
God will rebuild the Holy Temple
Speedily, speedily, in our days and soon.
Build it, Eternal One! Build it, Eternal One!

Distinguished is God, great is God, outstanding is God,
God will rebuild the Holy Temple
Speedily, speedily, in our days and soon.
Build it, Eternal One! Build it, Eternal One!

Resplendent is God, faithful is God, deserving is God, kind is God,
pure is God, unique is God, mighty is God, wise is God, sovereign is God,
awesome is God, sublime is God, strong is God, redeeming is God,
righteous is God, holy is God, merciful is God, almighty is God, resolute is God,

God will rebuild the Holy Temple
Speedily, speedily, in our days and soon.
Build it, Eternal One! Build it, Eternal One!

Eḥad Mi Yodei'a?

אֶחָד מִי יוֹדֵעַ? אֶחָד אֲנִי יוֹדֵעַ:
אֶחָד אֱלֹהֵינוּ שֶׁבַּשָּׁמַיִם וּבָאָרֶץ.

Eḥad mi yodei'a? Eḥad ani yodei'a:
Eḥad Eloheinu shebashamayim uva'aretz.

שְׁנַיִם מִי יוֹדֵעַ? שְׁנַיִם אֲנִי יוֹדֵעַ:
שְׁנֵי לֻחוֹת הַבְּרִית, אֶחָד אֱלֹהֵינוּ
שֶׁבַּשָּׁמַיִם וּבָאָרֶץ.

Sh'nayim mi yodei'a? Sh'nayim ani yodei'a:
Sh'nei luḥot habrit, eḥad Eloheinu
shebashamayim uva'aretz.

שְׁלֹשָׁה מִי יוֹדֵעַ? שְׁלֹשָׁה אֲנִי יוֹדֵעַ:
שְׁלֹשָׁה אָבוֹת, שְׁנֵי לֻחוֹת הַבְּרִית, אֶחָד
אֱלֹהֵינוּ שֶׁבַּשָּׁמַיִם וּבָאָרֶץ.

Sh'loshah mi yodei'a? Sh'loshah ani yodei'a:
Sh'loshah avot, sh'nei luḥot habrit, eḥad
Eloheinu shebashamayim uva'aretz.

אַרְבַּע מִי יוֹדֵעַ? אַרְבַּע אֲנִי יוֹדֵעַ:
אַרְבַּע אִמָּהוֹת, שְׁלֹשָׁה אָבוֹת, שְׁנֵי לֻחוֹת
הַבְּרִית, אֶחָד אֱלֹהֵינוּ שֶׁבַּשָּׁמַיִם וּבָאָרֶץ.

Arba mi yodei'a? Arba ani yodei'a:
Arba imahot, sh'loshah avot, sh'nei
luḥot habrit, eḥad Eloheinu shebashamayim
uva'aretz.

חֲמִשָּׁה מִי יוֹדֵעַ? חֲמִשָּׁה אֲנִי יוֹדֵעַ:
חֲמִשָּׁה חֻמְשֵׁי תוֹרָה, אַרְבַּע אִמָּהוֹת,
שְׁלֹשָׁה אָבוֹת, שְׁנֵי לֻחוֹת הַבְּרִית, אֶחָד
אֱלֹהֵינוּ שֶׁבַּשָּׁמַיִם וּבָאָרֶץ.

Ḥamishah mi yodei'a? Ḥamishah ani yodei'a:
Ḥamishah ḥum'shei Torah, arba imahot,
sh'loshah avot, sh'nei luḥot habrit, eḥad
Eloheinu shebashamayim uva'aretz.

שִׁשָּׁה מִי יוֹדֵעַ? שִׁשָּׁה אֲנִי יוֹדֵעַ:
שִׁשָּׁה סִדְרֵי מִשְׁנָה, חֲמִשָּׁה חֻמְשֵׁי
תוֹרָה, אַרְבַּע אִמָּהוֹת, שְׁלֹשָׁה אָבוֹת,
שְׁנֵי לֻחוֹת הַבְּרִית, אֶחָד אֱלֹהֵינוּ
שֶׁבַּשָּׁמַיִם וּבָאָרֶץ.

Shishah mi yodei'a? Shishah ani yodei'a:
Shishah sidrei Mishnah, ḥamishah ḥum'shei
Torah, arba imahot, sh'loshah avot, sh'nei
luḥot habrit, eḥad Eloheinu shebashamayim
uva'aretz.

שִׁבְעָה מִי יוֹדֵעַ? שִׁבְעָה אֲנִי יוֹדֵעַ:
שִׁבְעָה יְמֵי שַׁבְּתָא, שִׁשָּׁה סִדְרֵי מִשְׁנָה,
חֲמִשָּׁה חֻמְשֵׁי תוֹרָה, אַרְבַּע אִמָּהוֹת,
שְׁלֹשָׁה אָבוֹת, שְׁנֵי לֻחוֹת הַבְּרִית, אֶחָד
אֱלֹהֵינוּ שֶׁבַּשָּׁמַיִם וּבָאָרֶץ.

Shivah mi yodei'a? Shivah ani yodei'a:
Shivah y'mei Shabta, shishah sidrei
Mishnah, ḥamishah ḥum'shei Torah,
arba imahot, sh'loshah avot, sh'nei
luḥot habrit, eḥad Eloheinu
shebashamayim uva'aretz.

שְׁמוֹנָה מִי יוֹדֵעַ? שְׁמוֹנָה אֲנִי יוֹדֵעַ:
שְׁמוֹנָה יְמֵי מִילָה, שִׁבְעָה יְמֵי שַׁבְּתָא,
שִׁשָּׁה סִדְרֵי מִשְׁנָה, חֲמִשָּׁה חֻמְשֵׁי תוֹרָה,
אַרְבַּע אִמָּהוֹת, שְׁלֹשָׁה אָבוֹת, שְׁנֵי לֻחוֹת
הַבְּרִית, אֶחָד אֱלֹהֵינוּ שֶׁבַּשָּׁמַיִם וּבָאָרֶץ.

Sh'monah mi yodei'a? Sh'monah ani yodei'a: Sh'monah y'mei milah, shivah y'mei Shabta, shishah sidrei Mishnah, ḥamishah ḥum'shei Torah, arba imahot, sh'loshah avot, sh'nei luḥot habrit, eḥad Eloheinu shebashamayim uva'aretz.

תִּשְׁעָה מִי יוֹדֵעַ? תִּשְׁעָה אֲנִי יוֹדֵעַ:
תִּשְׁעָה יַרְחֵי לֵדָה, שְׁמוֹנָה יְמֵי מִילָה,
שִׁבְעָה יְמֵי שַׁבְּתָא, שִׁשָּׁה סִדְרֵי מִשְׁנָה,
חֲמִשָּׁה חֻמְשֵׁי תוֹרָה, אַרְבַּע אִמָּהוֹת,
שְׁלֹשָׁה אָבוֹת, שְׁנֵי לֻחוֹת הַבְּרִית, אֶחָד
אֱלֹהֵינוּ שֶׁבַּשָּׁמַיִם וּבָאָרֶץ.

Tishah mi yodei'a? Tishah ani yodei'a: Tishah yarḥei leidah, sh'monah y'mei milah, shivah y'mei Shabta, shishah sidrei Mishnah, ḥamishah ḥum'shei Torah, arba imahot, sh'loshah avot, sh'nei luḥot habrit, eḥad Eloheinu shebashamayim uva'aretz.

עֲשָׂרָה מִי יוֹדֵעַ? עֲשָׂרָה אֲנִי יוֹדֵעַ:
עֲשָׂרָה דִּבְּרַיָּא, תִּשְׁעָה יַרְחֵי לֵדָה, שְׁמוֹנָה
יְמֵי מִילָה, שִׁבְעָה יְמֵי שַׁבְּתָא, שִׁשָּׁה
סִדְרֵי מִשְׁנָה, חֲמִשָּׁה חֻמְשֵׁי תוֹרָה, אַרְבַּע
אִמָּהוֹת, שְׁלֹשָׁה אָבוֹת, שְׁנֵי לֻחוֹת הַבְּרִית,
אֶחָד אֱלֹהֵינוּ שֶׁבַּשָּׁמַיִם וּבָאָרֶץ.

Asarah mi yodei'a? Asarah ani yodei'a: Asarah dibraya, tishah yarḥei leidah, sh'monah y'mei milah, shivah y'mei Shabta, shishah sidrei Mishnah, ḥamishah ḥum'shei Torah, arba imahot, sh'loshah avot, sh'nei luḥot habrit, eḥad Eloheinu shebashamayim uva'aretz.

אַחַד עָשָׂר מִי יוֹדֵעַ? אַחַד עָשָׂר אֲנִי יוֹדֵעַ:
אַחַד עָשָׂר כּוֹכְבַיָּא, עֲשָׂרָה דִּבְּרַיָּא, תִּשְׁעָה
יַרְחֵי לֵדָה, שְׁמוֹנָה יְמֵי מִילָה, שִׁבְעָה
יְמֵי שַׁבְּתָא, שִׁשָּׁה סִדְרֵי מִשְׁנָה, חֲמִשָּׁה
חֻמְשֵׁי תוֹרָה, אַרְבַּע אִמָּהוֹת, שְׁלֹשָׁה
אָבוֹת, שְׁנֵי לֻחוֹת הַבְּרִית, אֶחָד אֱלֹהֵינוּ
שֶׁבַּשָּׁמַיִם וּבָאָרֶץ.

Aḥad asar mi yodei'a? Aḥad asar ani yodei'a: Aḥad asar kochvaya, asarah dibraya, tishah yarḥei leidah, sh'monah y'mei milah, shivah y'mei Shabta, shishah sidrei Mishnah, ḥamishah ḥum'shei Torah, arba imahot, sh'loshah avot, sh'nei luḥot habrit, eḥad Eloheinu shebashamayim uva'aretz.

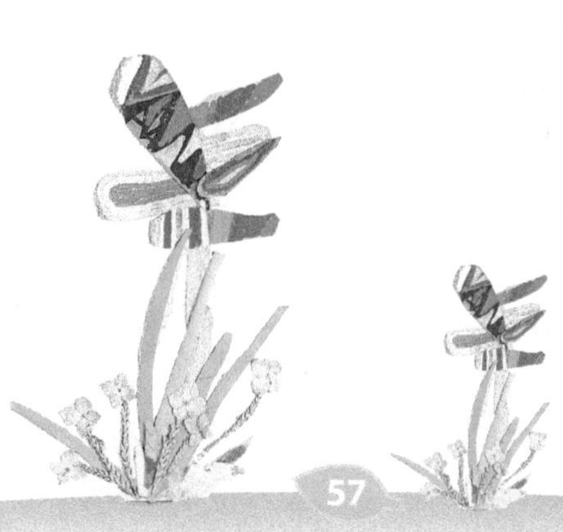

שְׁנֵים עָשָׂר מִי יוֹדֵעַ? שְׁנֵים עָשָׂר אֲנִי יוֹדֵעַ: שְׁנֵים עָשָׂר שִׁבְטַיָּא, אַחַד עָשָׂר כּוֹכְבַיָּא, עֲשָׂרָה דִּבְּרַיָּא, תִּשְׁעָה יַרְחֵי לֵדָה, שְׁמוֹנָה יְמֵי מִילָה, שִׁבְעָה יְמֵי שַׁבְּתָא, שִׁשָּׁה סִדְרֵי מִשְׁנָה, חֲמִשָּׁה חֻמְשֵׁי תוֹרָה, אַרְבַּע אִמָּהוֹת, שְׁלֹשָׁה אָבוֹת, שְׁנֵי לֻחוֹת הַבְּרִית, אֶחָד אֱלֹהֵינוּ שֶׁבַּשָּׁמַיִם וּבָאָרֶץ.

Sh'neim asar mi yodei'a? Sh'neim asar ani yodei'a: Sh'neim asar shivtaya, aḥad asar kochvaya, asarah dibraya, tishah yarḥei leidah, sh'monah y'mei milah, shivah y'mei Shabta, shishah sidrei Mishnah, ḥamishah ḥum'shei Torah, arba imahot, sh'loshah avot, sh'nei luḥot habrit, eḥad Eloheinu shebashamayim uva'aretz.

שְׁלֹשָׁה עָשָׂר מִי יוֹדֵעַ? שְׁלֹשָׁה עָשָׂר אֲנִי יוֹדֵעַ: שְׁלֹשָׁה עָשָׂר מִדַּיָּא, שְׁנֵים עָשָׂר שִׁבְטַיָּא, אַחַד עָשָׂר כּוֹכְבַיָּא, עֲשָׂרָה דִּבְּרַיָּא, תִּשְׁעָה יַרְחֵי לֵדָה, שְׁמוֹנָה יְמֵי מִילָה, שִׁבְעָה יְמֵי שַׁבְּתָא, שִׁשָּׁה סִדְרֵי מִשְׁנָה, חֲמִשָּׁה חֻמְשֵׁי תוֹרָה, אַרְבַּע אִמָּהוֹת, שְׁלֹשָׁה אָבוֹת, שְׁנֵי לֻחוֹת הַבְּרִית, אֶחָד אֱלֹהֵינוּ שֶׁבַּשָּׁמַיִם וּבָאָרֶץ.

Sh'loshah asar mi yodei'a? Sh'loshah asar ani yodei'a: Sh'loshah asar midaya, sh'neim asar shivtaya, aḥad asar kochvaya, asarah dibraya, tishah yarḥei leidah, sh'monah y'mei milah, shivah y'mei Shabta, shishah sidrei Mishnah, ḥamishah ḥum'shei Torah, arba imahot, sh'loshah avot, sh'nei luḥot habrit, eḥad Eloheinu shebashamayim uva'aretz.

Who knows one? I know one.
One is God in heaven and on earth.

Who knows two? I know two.
Two are the tablets of the Ten Commandments, and One is God in heaven and on earth.

Who knows three? I know three.
Three are the patriarchs, Two are the tablets of the Ten Commandments, and One is God in heaven and on earth.

Four are the matriarchs.
Five are the books of the Torah.
Six are the books of the Mishnah.
Seven are the days of the week.
Eight are the days to circumcision.
Nine are the months of pregnancy.
Ten are the Commandments.
Eleven are the stars of Joseph's dream.
Twelve are the tribes of Israel.
Thirteen are the attributes of God.

Ḥad Gadya

חַד גַּדְיָא, חַד גַּדְיָא, דִּזְבַן אַבָּא בִּתְרֵי זוּזֵי, חַד גַּדְיָא, חַד גַּדְיָא.

Ḥad gadya, ḥad gadya, dizvan aba bitrei zuzei, ḥad gadya, ḥad gadya.

וְאָתָא שׁוּנְרָא, וְאָכְלָה לְגַדְיָא, דִּזְבַן אַבָּא בִּתְרֵי זוּזֵי, חַד גַּדְיָא, חַד גַּדְיָא.

V'ata shun'ra, v'ach'lah l'gadya, dizvan aba bitrei zuzei, ḥad gadya, ḥad gadya.

וְאָתָא כַלְבָּא, וְנָשַׁךְ לְשׁוּנְרָא, דְּאָכְלָה לְגַדְיָא, דִּזְבַן אַבָּא בִּתְרֵי זוּזֵי, חַד גַּדְיָא, חַד גַּדְיָא.

V'ata chalba, v'nashach l'shun'ra, d'ach'lah l'gadya, dizvan aba bitrei zuzei, ḥad gadya, ḥad gadya.

וְאָתָא חוּטְרָא, וְהִכָּה לְכַלְבָּא, דְּנָשַׁךְ לְשׁוּנְרָא, דְּאָכְלָה לְגַדְיָא, דִּזְבַן אַבָּא בִּתְרֵי זוּזֵי, חַד גַּדְיָא, חַד גַּדְיָא.

V'ata ḥut'ra, v'hikah l'chalba, d'nashach l'shun'ra, d'ach'lah l'gadya, dizvan aba bitrei zuzei, ḥad gadya, ḥad gadya.

וְאָתָא נוּרָא, וְשָׂרַף לְחוּטְרָא, דְּהִכָּה לְכַלְבָּא, דְּנָשַׁךְ לְשׁוּנְרָא, דְּאָכְלָה לְגַדְיָא, דִּזְבַן אַבָּא בִּתְרֵי זוּזֵי, חַד גַּדְיָא, חַד גַּדְיָא.

V'ata nura, v'saraf l'ḥut'ra, d'hikah l'chalba, d'nashach l'shun'ra, d'ach'lah l'gadya, dizvan aba bitrei zuzei, ḥad gadya, ḥad gadya.

וְאָתָא מַיָּא, וְכָבָה לְנוּרָא, דְּשָׂרַף לְחוּטְרָא, דְּהִכָּה לְכַלְבָּא, דְּנָשַׁךְ לְשׁוּנְרָא, דְּאָכְלָה לְגַדְיָא, דִּזְבַן אַבָּא בִּתְרֵי זוּזֵי, חַד גַּדְיָא, חַד גַּדְיָא.

V'ata maya, v'chavah l'nura, d'saraf l'ḥut'ra, d'hikah l'chalba, d'nashach l'shun'ra, d'ach'lah l'gadya, dizvan aba bitrei zuzei, ḥad gadya, ḥad gadya.

V'ata tora, v'shata l'maya, d'chava l'nura, d'saraf l'ḥut'ra, d'hikah l'chalba, d'nashach l'shun'ra, d'achlah l'gadya, dizvan aba bitrei zuzei, ḥad gadya, ḥad gadya.

וְאָתָא תוֹרָא, וְשָׁתָא לְמַיָּא, דְּכָבָה
לְנוּרָא, דְּשָׂרַף לְחוּטְרָא, דְּהִכָּה
לְכַלְבָּא, דְּנָשַׁךְ לְשׁוּנְרָא, דְּאָכְלָה
לְגַדְיָא, דִּזְבַן אַבָּא בִּתְרֵי זוּזֵי, חַד
גַּדְיָא, חַד גַּדְיָא.

V'ata hashoḥeit, v'shaḥat l'tora, d'shata l'maya, d'chavah l'nura, d'saraf l'ḥut'ra, d'hikah l'chalba, d'nashach l'shun'ra, d'ach'lah l'gadya, dizvan aba bitrei zuzei, ḥad gadya, ḥad gadya.

וְאָתָא הַשּׁוֹחֵט, וְשָׁחַט לְתוֹרָא,
דְּשָׁתָא לְמַיָּא, דְּכָבָה לְנוּרָא, דְּשָׂרַף
לְחוּטְרָא, דְּהִכָּה לְכַלְבָּא, דְּנָשַׁךְ
לְשׁוּנְרָא, דְּאָכְלָה לְגַדְיָא, דִּזְבַן אַבָּא
בִּתְרֵי זוּזֵי, חַד גַּדְיָא, חַד גַּדְיָא.

V'ata malach hamavet, v'shaḥat l'shoḥeit, d'shaḥat l'tora, d'shata l'maya, d'chavah l'nura, d'saraf l'ḥut'ra, d'hikah l'chalba, d'nashach l'shun'ra, d'ach'lah l'gadya, dizvan aba bitrei zuzei, ḥad gadya, ḥad gadya.

וְאָתָא מַלְאַךְ הַמָּוֶת, וְשָׁחַט לַשּׁוֹחֵט,
דְּשָׁחַט לְתוֹרָא, דְּשָׁתָא לְמַיָּא, דְּכָבָה
לְנוּרָא, דְּשָׂרַף לְחוּטְרָא, דְּהִכָּה
לְכַלְבָּא, דְּנָשַׁךְ לְשׁוּנְרָא, דְּאָכְלָה
לְגַדְיָא, דִּזְבַן אַבָּא בִּתְרֵי זוּזֵי, חַד
גַּדְיָא, חַד גַּדְיָא.

V'ata haKadosh Baruch Hu, v'shaḥat l'malach hamavet, d'shaḥat l'shoḥeit, d'shaḥat l'tora, d'shata l'maya, d'chavah l'nura, d'saraf l'ḥut'ra, d'hikah l'chalba, d'nashach l'shun'ra, d'ach'lah l'gadya, dizvan aba bitrei zuzei, ḥad gadya, ḥad gadya.

וְאָתָא הַקָּדוֹשׁ בָּרוּךְ הוּא, וְשָׁחַט
לְמַלְאַךְ הַמָּוֶת, דְּשָׁחַט לַשּׁוֹחֵט,
דְּשָׁחַט לְתוֹרָא, דְּשָׁתָא לְמַיָּא, דְּכָבָה
לְנוּרָא, דְּשָׂרַף לְחוּטְרָא, דְּהִכָּה
לְכַלְבָּא, דְּנָשַׁךְ לְשׁוּנְרָא, דְּאָכְלָה
לְגַדְיָא, דִּזְבַן אַבָּא בִּתְרֵי זוּזֵי, חַד
גַּדְיָא, חַד גַּדְיָא.

One little goat, one little goat,
My father bought for two zuzim,
Ḥad gadya, ḥad gadya.

Along came the cat and ate the goat my father bought for two zuzim, *ḥad gadya ḥad gadya.*

Then came the dog and bit the cat that ate the goat my father bought for two zuzim, *ḥad gadya ḥad gadya.*

Then came the stick and hit the dog that bit the cat that ate the goat my father bought for two zuzim, *ḥad gadya ḥad gadya.*

Then came the fire and burned the stick that hit the dog that bit the cat that ate the goat my father bought for two zuzim, *ḥad gadya ḥad gadya.*

Then came the water and quenched the fire that burned the stick that hit the dog that bit the cat that ate the goat my father bought for two zuzim, *ḥad gadya ḥad gadya.*

Then came the ox and drank the water that quenched the fire that burned the stick that hit the dog that bit the cat that ate the goat my father bought for two zuzim, *ḥad gadya ḥad gadya.*

Then came the butcher and killed the ox that drank the water that quenched the fire that burned the stick that hit the dog that bit the cat that ate the goat my father bought for two zuzim, *ḥad gadya ḥad gadya.*

Then came the angel of death and slew the butcher that killed the ox that drank the water that quenched the fire that burned the stick that hit the dog that bit the cat that ate the goat my father bought for two zuzim, *ḥad gadya ḥad gadya.*

Then came the Holy One, praised be God, and destroyed the angel of death that slew the butcher that killed the ox that drank the water that quenched the fire that burned the stick that hit the dog that bit the cat that ate the goat my father bought for two zuzim, *ḥad gadya, ḥad gadya!*

Activities to Enrich Your Seder

1. **Afikoman envelope.** Decorate a large envelope to look like a piece of matzah, and write the word *afikoman* in the center. The leader can place the afikoman into this envelope before hiding it.
2. **Place cards and napkin rings.** Ask children to make place cards with your guests' names, or napkin rings cut from cardboard towel rolls. Decorate the cards and rings with Passover themes, using gift wrap, paint, markers, or stencils.
3. **Question box.** Decorate a shoe box with question marks and prepare questions about Passover on small cards to put in the box. Ask seder participants to each pull out a question and try to answer it. Seder participants can help each other answer questions as well.
4. **Passover skit.** Help children prepare a skit in advance, to tell the story of Passover. Collect costumes and props, and consider using dolls or finger puppets to tell the story.

5. **Mini-dramas.** Ask participants to act out these mini-dramas, being sure to show how the character feels:
    - Moses in front of the powerful Pharaoh
    - A Hebrew slave scared by the plagues
    - A Hebrew slave being told to hurry up and pack to leave Egypt *now!*
6. **Personal stories.** Ask each participant to share a personal or family story of liberation or journey to freedom. You might want to ask this in advance, to give guests time to think about what they would like to share.
7. **Ḥaroset tasting.** Prepare different types of ḥaroset based on recipes from around the world, or invite guests to make and bring their own ḥaroset recipes. Let everyone taste a little of each and discuss their reactions to the different flavors.

Topics for Discussion

Redemption of Captives

Jewish law teaches that the redemption of captives is a *mitzvah rabbah*, a "great commandment," taking precedence over giving money and clothing to the needy or any other mitzvah. (*Yoreh Dei'ah* 252:1)

1. Why do you think rescuing captives takes precedence over other *mitzvot* (plural of mitzvah)?
2. In what circumstances would you expose yourself to danger in order to save another person's life?

Slavery Versus Freedom

The haggadah teaches us that: "We were slaves to Pharaoh in Egypt, but God took us out from there with a mighty hand and an outstretched arm."

1. At what other times were Jews persecuted or discriminated against?
2. Think of some groups of people who suffer from persecution or discrimination today. What can you do to help?

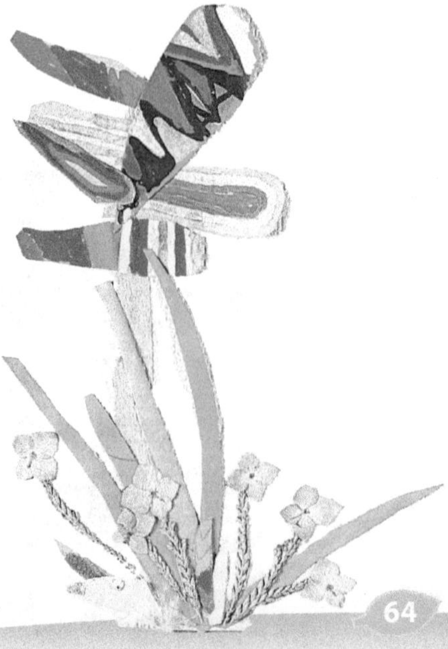